Now Hear This! SCIENCE

Activities to Improve Science and Listening Skills

by Ann Richmond Fisher

Illustrated by Mike Artell

Teaching & Learning Company

1204 Buchanan St., P.O. Box 10
Carthage, IL 62321-0010

Cover art © Corel Corporation

Copyright © 1999, Teaching & Learning Company

ISBN No. 1-57310-182-6

Printing No. 987654321

Teaching & Learning Company
1204 Buchanan St., P.O. Box 10
Carthage, IL 62321-0010

The purchase of this book entitles teachers to make copies for use in their individual classrooms, only. This book, or any part of it, may not be reproduced in any form for any other purposes without prior written permission from the Teaching & Learning Company. It is strictly prohibited to reproduce any part of this book for an entire school or school district, or for commercial resale.

All rights reserved. Printed in the United States of America.

This book belongs to

_____

Dedication

This book is dedicated to my good friends in Ireland,
to those on both sides of the border.
May the Emerald Isle soon be blessed with peace.

Table of Contents

Computers 9
Energy 23
Water 39
Animals 52
The Human Body 65
The Solar System 78
Answer Key 90

Dear Teacher or Parent,

This is a resource you'll turn to repeatedly as you study science with your middle-grade students. This is really two books in one—a *science* book that contains topics ranging from calories to computers—and, a *listening* book that stretches skills in hearing and following directions. As you use the activities in this book, you are building students' science knowledge and listening abilities simultaneously. There is no need to take time away from this important content area while you teach good listening habits!

Many important science skills are covered in this book. The lessons are arranged by general topics as listed in the table of contents. Topics include computers, energy, water, animals, the human body and the solar system. Specific skills covered in each lesson appear in the top corner of the page. Usually easier lessons are placed first in each section. It is suggested that you begin with easier lessons so that the students' focus will first be on listening. You may also want to repeat directions two or three times in the beginning. Eventually, you will be able to move on to harder skills with less teacher help. The wide range of activities will keep your students interested and listening!

This book is a complete resource which contains everything from pretests to a chart for recording student progress. Lessons require little preparation on the part of the teacher. For many of the lessons, your students will need only a piece of paper and pencil. For others you will need to photocopy a reproducible page. Materials needed are always listed in the top corner of the lesson, so you can see what is needed at a glance. An answer key is provided in the back of the book which will help you check students' results quickly.

The page that follows, "How to Use This Book," contains more specific instructions on using special features of this book. It is our goal to provide appealing, helpful lessons for you, the classroom teacher, as you seek to train your students in language and listening!

Sincerely,

Ann

Ann Richmond Fisher

How to Use This Book

To get maximum benefit from the various features of this book, use the suggestions that follow.

Warm-Ups: These are fun activities at the beginning of each section that will introduce students to the upcoming content area. The purpose of the warm-ups is not only to give students a sample of the work ahead but also to get students excited about it.

Pre/Posttests: These have been written to help the teacher evaluate student progress. The teacher should carefully preview the upcoming unit before administering the pretest. If some lessons are inappropriate for your class (i.e. too difficult or too easy), then there may also be inappropriate items on the pre/posttest. Feel free to use only the questions on the tests that correspond to lessons in the unit you will actually be using. Come up with your own number for the highest possible test score. Use the **Teacher Record Page** to record the date of each pretest, the number of items on the test and each student's score. After the class completes all appropriate lessons in the unit, administer the same test again, and record student scores for the posttest on the record page. At a glance you can see which students are making significant progress in their listening and science skills. If some students are not improving, try to work with them individually or in small groups to diagnose any problems they may be having.

Lessons: Most lessons are written so that you can read them to an entire class while each student completes one page of work. You can then collect the work and evaluate it using the **Answer Key** in the back of the book. Or students can check their own work as the entire class works through the correct solution together. **Important:** In each lesson students are instructed where to write their names on the paper. Make sure they wait and listen to these instructions. Also note that for some lessons, student outcomes can vary from the answers shown and still be acceptable.

Although the lessons can be administered in a traditional manner described above, some can also be adapted to other formats. A few ideas are listed below. Use your imagination and try other ideas of your own as well.

Cooperative Learning Groups: Some activities can be completed in pairs or small work groups. This requires students to agree on what they've heard and to work together on their outcomes. "More Keyboarding" (page 14), "Burning Up!" (page 33), "River Route" (page 45) and others are suited to this format.

Chalkboard Lessons: "Sarah's Source" (page 24), "Fractured Mammals" (page 58), "Bone Fractures" (page 69) and many others written on plain paper can be done at the chalkboard. You may wish to have three or four students at the chalkboard while the rest work at their seats. This will allow you to spot problems immediately. The chalkboard worker may be distracting to the others; students will need to listen and concentrate even harder.

Remind students that other answers may be possible, or they may be incorrect. Emphasize the need for each student to do his own best work.

Team Relays: For "Four Forms" (page 28), "A Beating Heart" (page 75), " 'Organ'ization!" (page 76) and others, try this. Divide the class into teams of four to six students each. Have one member from each team go to the board and solve one problem, have the second member of the team do the next one and so on. All along the way, the team needs to listen carefully to be sure instructions are followed. Allow one person from each team to have the opportunity to correct earlier mistakes.

Content Variations: For many lessons, the content can easily be changed while retaining the format and instructions. Such lessons include "In and Out" (page 15), "No Bones About It!" (page 54) and "Astronomical Matchup" (page 89).

Teacher Record Page

Student Name	# possible	Pretest 1	Posttest 1	Pretest 2	Posttest 2	Pretest 3	Posttest 3	Pretest 4	Posttest 4	Pretest 5	Posttest 5	Pretest 6	Posttest 6
Date													

PRE/POSTTEST FOR PART 1

Computers

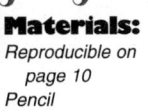
Materials:
Reproducible on page 10
Pencil

Write your name in the top right corner of your page.

For numbers 1 to 3, listen to the statements I will read. Decide whether they describe a computer or a person. Circle the correct word for each one.

1. It does the same task in a slightly different way each time.
2. It can choose when it wants to perform which one of several different jobs.
3. It can work consistently with huge amounts of information.

Questions 4 to 6 refer to the computer keyboard.

4. The keys YUIOP all appear together on the keyboard. Are they on the top, middle or bottom row of letters on the keyboard? Circle the correct word.
5. The letters ZQAST are all on the same side of the keyboard. Should you type them with your left hand or your right hand? Circle the answer.
6. What do you call the middle row of letters, where your hands should rest? Write the name in the blank at number 6.

Now look at the Input/Output Table. Write in the rule in the top box and then complete the rest of the table.

Rule: Vowels are worth 1 point; consonants are worth 2 points. Find the total points for each word.

7. Input is DOG. Find the output.
8. Input is BUTTER. Find the output.
9. Output is 7. Find one input.

Now look at the spreadsheet at number 10. Supply these numbers: cell B2-14, cell A3-17, cell C4-24, cell C2-11, cell B1-10.

Now write the sum of cells C1 through C4 in C6. Write the sum of A2 through C2 in D2.

Next look at the data in the box. Think of three different ways a computer could sort this information. Write three methods on the lines at numbers 11 to 13. For each method, also tell who would be first on the list.

For numbers 14 to 16, write the letters I read to you in the first blank by each number. Then unscramble the letters to spell a common computer term and write that in the second blank.

14. sumoe
15. adta asbe
16. morgrap

PRE/POSTTEST FOR PART 1

Computers

1. Computer   Person
2. Computer   Person
3. Computer   Person
4. Top   Middle   Bottom
5. Left   Right
6. _____

Input/Output Table

Rule:	
Input	**Output**
7.	
8.	
9.	

10. Spreadsheet

	A	B	C	D	E
1	13		15		
2	25				
3		17	13		
4	26	21			
5					
6					

White	12/25/60	Doctor	Mesa, AZ	85364
Bond	7/11/75	Salesperson	Dallas, TX	75260
Stone	6/20/49	Nurse	Cleveland, OH	44101

11. _____
12. _____
13. _____
14. _____   _____
15. _____   _____
16. _____   _____

COMPUTERS

Man or Machine?

Skills: Analyzing human ability versus computer skills

Materials: Just students

Use as a warm-up for Part 1.

Computers do a lot of work very quickly, but in some situations humans are still better. As I read each statement, decide if it best describes a person or a computer. If you think it describes a person, raise your hand. If you think it describes a computer, stand up. We will discuss your answers as we go.

(Teacher: Suggested answers are indicated with a P [person] or a C [computer], although students may be able to justify the opposite choice. In general, they should conclude that people are best at flexibility, creativity and perceptiveness. Computers are best at precision, predictability, speed and handling large amounts of data.)

1. It can choose when it wants to perform which one of several different jobs. (P)
2. It always calculates the correct answer. (C)
3. It requires a small amount of space to store a lot of information. (C)
4. It can change its direction partway through a task and then continue in a different way. (P)
5. It can make a creative, new solution to an old problem. (P)
6. It can recall each piece of information it has received. (C)
7. It does the same task in a slightly different way each time. (P)
8. It is predictable. (C)
9. It can express impatience when it encounters difficulty with a task. (P)
10. It can work consistently with huge amounts of information. (C)

(Teacher: Encourage students to add more statements to the list for others to analyze.)

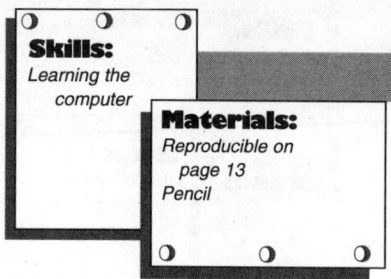

COMPUTERS

Complete the Keyboard

In this lesson we will work on learning the placement of letters on the computer keyboard. We will also work on the best placement of your fingers while learning to type. Begin by writing your name in the top right corner of the worksheet. To help you not get confused later on, also label the right and left sides of your sheet. Write *left* near the top of the page on the left-hand side. Write the word *right* near the top on the right-hand side.

1. Look at the keyboard on your worksheet. The middle row of keys is where your hands should rest. It is called the "home row." Write the words *home row* to the left of the keyboard, near the middle row.

2. Now fill in the missing letters for the home row. Begin on the left, where the first letter is A. Next are S, D, F and G. After the G draw a short diagonal line to separate the letters typed by the left hand from those typed by the right hand. Then completing the home row keys, fill in the letters H, J, K and L.

3. You can see that there are 10 keys shown on your page in the home row. Since your thumbs don't rest on any keys while typing, there are obviously two extra keys in this row. The G and H are used by stretching the index finger of each hand. Use your pencil to shade in the other eight keys in the home row, showing where your eight fingers should rest. This includes the colon/semicolon key.

4. Now complete the missing letters in the top row which begin with Q. The missing letters in order are W, E, R, T, Y, U, I, O and P. Draw a diagonal line between the T and Y to separate the left-hand keys from the right-hand keys.

5. Now complete the bottom row which begins with Z. The missing letters are X, C, V, B, N and M. Draw a short diagonal line between the B and N to separate the left-hand keys from the right-hand keys.

(Teacher: Stop here for a shorter lesson, or continue on to page 14 for more practice with the keyboard. This second part can also be done at a later time, provided the students keep their reproducibles.)

Keyboard

Reproducible for use with pages 12 and 14.

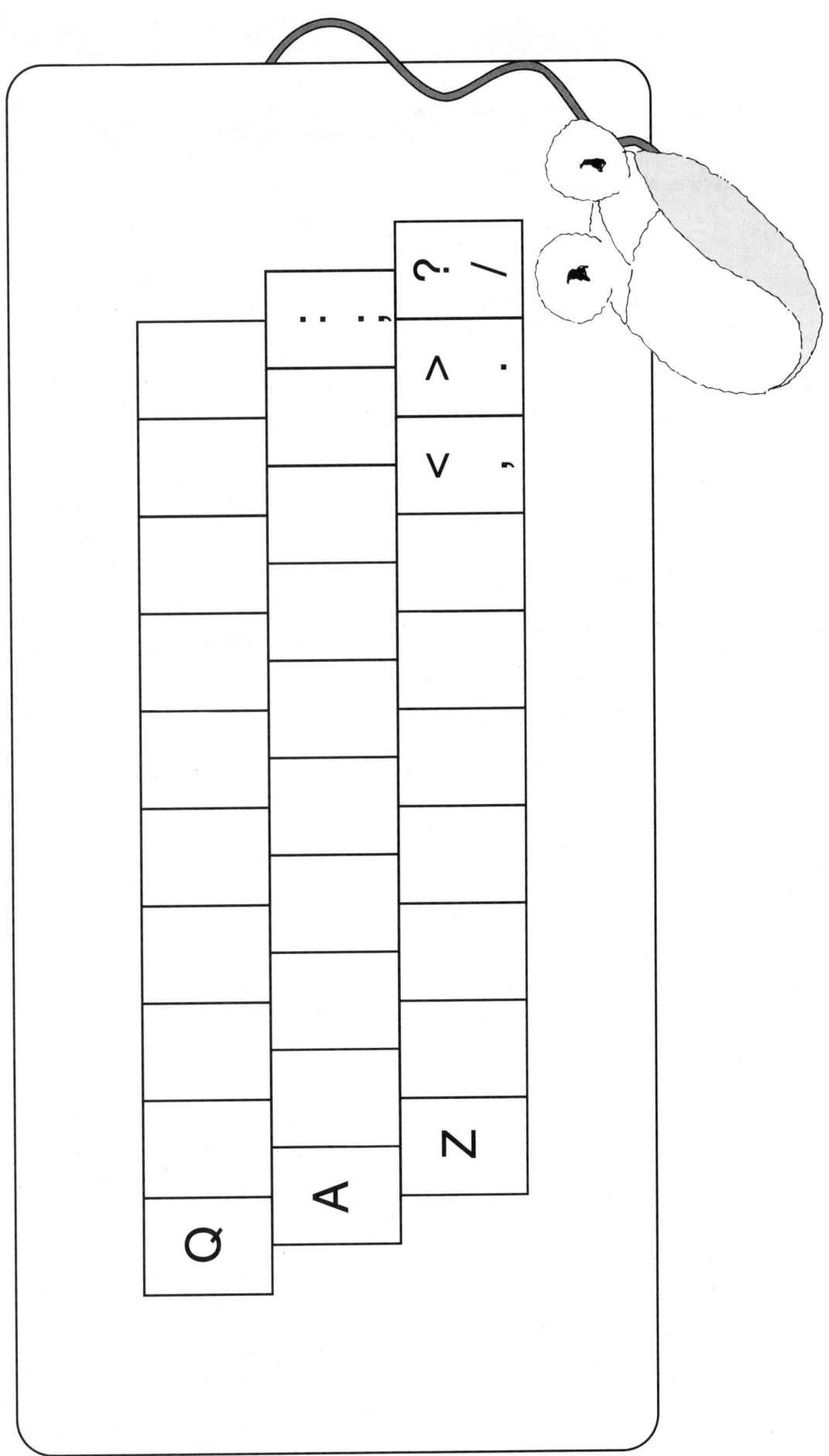

TLC10182 Copyright © Teaching & Learning Company, Carthage, IL 62321-0010

COMPUTERS

More Keyboarding

Skills: Locating letters on a keyboard

Materials: Completed reproducible from pages 12 and 13; Pencil

Underneath the keyboard, number from 1 to 12. Follow my directions for each number.

1. On line 1, print your first name. Look at the keyboard to see if you should use your left hand, your right hand or both hands to type your first name correctly. Next to your name write *left, right* or *both*.

2. On line 2, print your last name. Look at the keyboard to see if you should use your left hand, your right hand or both hands to type your last name correctly. Next to your name write *left, right* or *both*.

3. On line 3, print a three-letter word that follows this pattern: left hand, right hand, left hand.

4. On line 4, print a three-letter word that follows the pattern right hand, left hand, right hand.

5. Now find a three-letter word typed completely with the left hand.

6. Find a three-letter word typed completely with the right hand.

7. Find two words of any length typed completely with home row keys.

8. Write a four-letter word that follows this pattern: left, right, right, left.

9. Write a four-letter word that follows this pattern: right, right, left, left.

10. Find two words of any length typed completely with top row keys.

11. Find a word of four or more letters spelled with only right-hand keys.

12. Find a word of four or more letters spelled with only left-hand keys.

14

TLC10182 Copyright © Teaching & Learning Company, Carthage, IL 62321-0010

COMPUTERS

In and Out

Skills: Understanding input and output

Materials: Reproducible on page 17
Pencil

For many computer programs, information is put into the program, a rule is applied to it and an answer comes out. The *input* and *output* can be shown on a screen or printout. On your worksheet are four tables for input and output.

Table 1

Look at table 1. The rule is printed in the top box. For each line in the table, I will read you either the input or the output. Your job is to use the rule and supply the missing information. For example, write the number 3 for the input on the example line. What will the output be? Yes, the answer is 11. Write 11 in the output part of the example. Now continue in the same manner.

Line 1: The input is 7. Find the output.
Line 2: The input is 11. Find the output.
Line 3: The input is 25. Find the output.
Line 4: The output is 14. What was the input?
Line 5: The output is 32. What was the input?

Table 2

Rule: Vowels are worth 2 points; consonants are worth 1 point. Find the total points for each word. For example, write the word *cat* as the input. What will the output be?

Yes, 4. Now continue.

Line 6: Input is *broom*. Find the output.
Line 7: Input is *yellow*. Find the output.
Line 8: Input is *nothing*. Find the output.
Line 9: Output is 3. What is one possible input?
Line 10: Output is 5. What is one possible input?

Table 3

Rule: Replace each letter with the one before it in the alphabet.
11. Input: VQ. Find the output.
12. Input: SBU. Find the output.
13. Input: MJLF. Find the output.
14. Output: OLD. Find the input.
15. Output: FROG. Find the input.

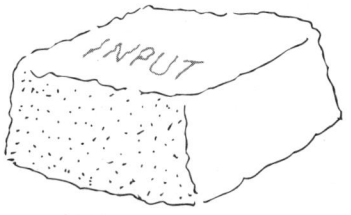

15

TLC10182 Copyright © Teaching & Learning Company, Carthage, IL 62321-0010

COMPUTERS

In and Out

Table 4

Rule: Divide by 4, add 1.
16. Input: 12. Find the output.
17. Input: 20. Find the output.
18. Input: 40. Find the output.
19. Output: 8. Find the input.
20. Output: 10. Find the input.

Table 5

You need to figure out the rule, based on the information I give you.
21. Input: 16, output: 5
22. Input: 25, output: 8
23. Input: 100, output: 33

Now try to figure out the rule and complete the last two lines.
24. Input: 13. What is the output?
25. Input: 40. What is the output?

Table 6

You need to figure out the rule again.
26. Input: MO, output: TU
27. Input: FR, output: SA
28. Input: WE, output: TH

Now try to figure out the rule and complete the last two lines.
29. Input: SU. What is the output?
30. Input: TH. What is the output?

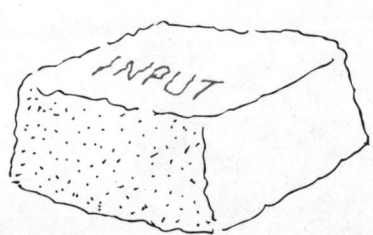
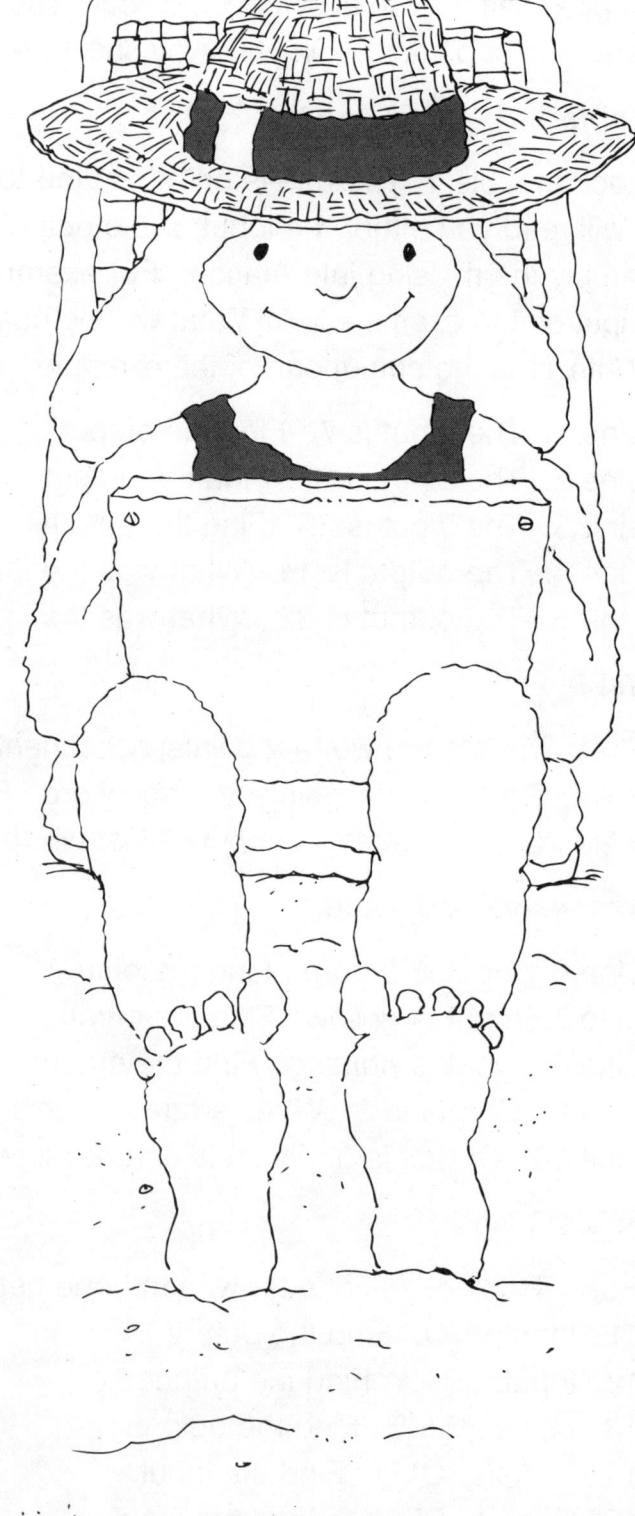

In and Out

Reproducible for use with pages 15 and 16.

Table 1
Multiply by 3, add 2.

Input	Output
ex.	
1.	
2.	
3.	
4.	
5.	

Table 2

Input	Output
ex.	
6.	
7.	
8.	
9.	
10.	

Table 3

Input	Output
11.	
12.	
13.	
14.	
15.	

Table 4

Input	Output
16.	
17.	
18.	
19.	
20.	

Table 5

Input	Output
21.	
22.	
23.	
24.	
25.	

Table 6

Input	Output
26.	
27.	
28.	
29.	
30.	

TLC10182 Copyright © Teaching & Learning Company, Carthage, IL 62321-0010

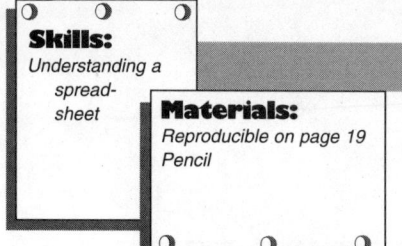

C O M P U T E R S

Spread It!

In this lesson you will learn a little bit about how spreadsheets work. On your worksheet you will see that there are rows labeled with numbers and columns that are labeled with letters. This divides the page into little boxes called cells. Cells can be filled with letters or numbers. Each cell can be identified by the number and letter of its location. For example, the first cell in the upper left-hand corner of the spreadsheet is cell A1. Print your name in cells A1 and B1. Write today's date in F1.

Now we'll do a simple spreadsheet, similar to one an accountant might use. We will use it to tally the number of school lunches ordered by four classrooms in one week. Skip down to cell A5. Write the word *class* in the cell. In cells B5 through F5 write the days of the week, Monday through Friday.

In column A, we'll now write the names of the teachers whose classes ordered lunches. In A6 write *Smith*, in A7 write *Jones,* in A8 write *Green* and in A9 write *Brown.* Now I will read you the numbers of lunches ordered and the cells in which to place the numbers. I will purposely skip around, so listen carefully!

C7–25	D9–15	F7–22
D6–22	B8–20	E6–20
B9–18	F9–14	C8–15
E8–20	E7–21	F8–16
F6–21	D8–18	C6–24
B7–23	B6–22	E9–13
C9–20	D7–20	

Now go back and make a brief title for this chart. Use the empty cells in row 3.

Once you have this information entered on the computer, you can find totals very easily. You could click on cell B10, type in a command to find the sum of cells B6 through B9, press "Enter," and the sum would appear instantly. However, since your worksheet is not a computer, use addition to find the total of lunches ordered on Monday. Write your sum in cell B10.

Now find the total number of lunches ordered on Tuesday. Write the sum in C10. Next find out how many lunches were ordered for the week by Mr. Smith's class. Write the total in G6.

Finally, find the week's total ordered by Ms. Brown's class. Write the total in G9.

Spread It!

Reproducible for use with page 18.

	A	B	C	D	E	F	G
1							
2							
3							
4							
5							
6							
7							
8							
9							
10							

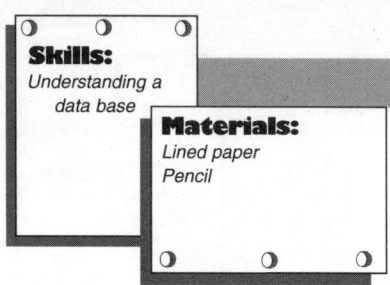

Skills: Understanding a data base

Materials: Lined paper, Pencil

COMPUTERS

Data Details

In this lesson you will learn how a computer data base works. A data base is used to store, sort and retrieve information. For instance, a salesperson might keep information on all of his or her clients including name, address, phone number, favorite products, best time of day to call and so on. Data bases often contain very large amounts of data, perhaps for thousands of customers. The computer can be asked to sort the information in many different ways, such as alphabetically by last name, by geographical area or by birth date.

To give you a better idea of how a data base can work, we will now write a small one on our own and sort through some of the information it contains. Starting on the second line of your page, number your paper from 1 to 10 skipping a line between numbers. To fit in all the information you will need to keep your writing small and neat. Use the extra line between numbers, if necessary, for extra space. Above your numbers, on the top line, print these five headings: Name, Date of Birth (abbreviated DOB, if you like), Profession, City/State and ZIP.

Now I will read you data for 10 customers. Listen carefully and copy the information accurately on your page. Use the two-letter abbreviation for the names of states, which I will give you. Ask if you need help on any other spellings.

Name	DOB	Profession	City/State	Zip
1. Long	9/21/35	Doctor	Atlanta, GA	30304
2. Rich	9/30/66	Accountant	Detroit, MI	48233
3. White	12/25/60	Doctor	Mesa, AZ	85364
4. Bond	7/11/75	Salesperson	Dallas, TX	75260
5. Stone	6/20/49	Nurse	Cleveland, OH	44101
6. Yates	6/13/72	Police Officer	Boulder, CO	80302
7. Fisher	9/6/58	Teacher	South Bend, IN	46616
8. Miller	9/25/36	Lawyer	Lansing, MI	48924
9. Ball	6/19/70	Pharmacist	Largo, FL	33540
10. Brown	4/25/38	Salesperson	Canton, OH	44711

COMPUTERS

Data Details

Under your list of information number from 1 to 17. Answer the questions I give you for each line. In many cases you will need to answer two or three parts. Write your answers all on the same line, in the same order as the directions.

11. Suppose you were to ask the computer to sort these people alphabetically by last name. Write the name of the person who would come first. Beside it write the name of the one who would come last.

12. An auto insurance company wants to send a mailing to all people living in a certain geographical area. It sends letters to those in ZIP codes beginning with 42 through 49, arranging clients in numerical order by ZIP code. Write the name of the person who would be first. Beside it write the name of the person who would be last. How many people in all from your list would receive the mailing?

13. A restaurant owner wants to send a coupon for a free dinner to anyone having a birthday in September. She wants to send them out in chronological order by date in the month. How many people on the list would receive a coupon? Who would be first? Who would be last?

14. A drug company wants to send an advertisement for a new medicine to all health care workers. How many people from this list should receive the ad? If they are arranged alphabetically by last name, who would be first? Who would be last?

15. A senior citizens group wants to invite anyone over age 60 to attend a party. How many people from this list should be invited? If arranged from oldest to youngest, who would be first? Who would be last?

16. If these people were arranged alphabetically by state, who would be first? Who would be last?

17. Two people are from the same state. The computer would have to be told how to decide which comes first. What would you suggest?

This should give you an idea of how computer data bases work. Imagine trying to answer these questions when looking through a list of 5000 customers! The computer can do it quickly, provided it has been supplied with the right instructions.

Skills: Recognizing common computer terms

Materials: Lined paper, Pencil

C O M P U T E R S

Computer Scramble

Number your paper from 1 to 15. Write your name on line 1. For the other numbers I will read to you a set of letters which you should write on your paper. Next to these letters, write a common computer word that can be spelled by unscrambling those letters.

(Teacher: Depending on the knowledge and experience of your students, you may also want to read the definitions written below as "hints" for each word.)

2. suome–a device that you roll around on a desk to move an on-screen pointer
3. tipun–information going into the computer
4. wradhear–all the computer equipment, including all the input and output devices
5. domem–a device which makes it possible for computers to communicate with one another over the telephone lines
6. scid–a magnetic storage object for computer information
7. trenrip–a device that can print out words and pictures from a computer
8. siruv–an error introduced to a computer or software to purposely cause problems
9. nyriba–the number system used by computers based on a 0 and 1
10. aatd seab–a program that stores information in such a way that it can be retrieved very quickly
11. frowsate–computer programs on disc, tape or CD-ROM
12. omparrg–a set of instructions that tell the computer what to do
13. ryemom–the chips in the computer where information and instructions are stored
14. thawflocr–a chart showing the steps needed for a computer program
15. begtamey–a measure of data storage, larger than a million bytes

PRE/POSTTEST FOR PART 2

Energy

Materials:
Lined paper
Pencil

Write your name in the top right corner of your page. Number your paper from 1 to 14. Write your answer for each number as I read the question.

1. List five things in your home that run on electricity.

2. I will read four steps in the process of producing electricity. The steps will be labeled A, B, C and D. Write the letters on line 2 in the order that the steps occur.

    A. Inside the generator, the magnet or the coil of wire turns which produces electricity.

    B. Steam turns turbines that operate generators.

    C. The electrical current goes to a transformer, where the voltage is increased.

    D. Coal is burned in a power station to boil water.

3. Does a moving bicycle have potential energy or kinetic energy? Write P or K.

4. Does a rock at the top of a hill have potential energy or kinetic energy? Write P or K.

For the next three numbers, write *true* or *false*.

5. Mechanical energy is the energy of moving objects.

6. Thermal energy that flows from an object is heat.

7. Your body releases radiant energy.

For numbers 8 through 12, write the word that belongs in each blank.

8. The chemical energy in foods is measured in units called _____.

9. If you don't take in enough calories, you will _____ weight.

10. If you take in more calories than you use, the energy is stored in your body as _____.

11. Wind energy can be used over and over again so it is called a _____ energy source.

12. An important scientific principle about energy says that energy cannot be created or _____.

13. Name one thing people do that wastes energy.

14. Name one thing we can do to save energy.

TLC10182 Copyright © Teaching & Learning Company, Carthage, IL 62321-0010

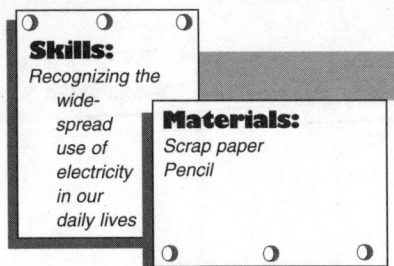

Skills: Recognizing the widespread use of electricity in our daily lives

Materials: Scrap paper, Pencil

ENERGY

Sarah's Source

Use as a warm-up for Part 2.

I will read you a short story about a girl named Sarah. You need to listen carefully and make a tally mark every time you hear me refer to something that uses electricity.

Story

Sarah awakened at 6:30 a.m. to the sound of her alarm clock radio. After listening to one song, she turned off the radio and got out of bed. She ran down the hallway and headed for the bathroom where she took a nice, hot shower. Afterwards, she got dressed and dried her hair. While she waited for her curling iron to heat, she went downstairs for breakfast.

In the kitchen, Sarah's brother was already eating.

"There's orange juice in the fridge," said Ken. "I'm having toaster waffles, and there are more for you, if you like. "I'm also making hot chocolate in the microwave."

After helping herself to the juice, hot chocolate and waffles, Sarah placed all the dirty dishes in the dishwasher. She folded a load of towels from the dryer that had finished drying last night and started a load of sheets in the washer while she listened in with her dad to the morning television newscast.

With the chores out of her way, Sarah returned to her room and flipped on the light. She put on a CD and listened to her favorite group while she curled her hair. By the time she was finished, the doorbell rang. It was her friend Mindy, who was ready to walk to school with Sarah.

Now count up your tally marks. Write the number of electrical items you heard mentioned in the story. Compare your number with other students. Then listen again to the story to see if your number needs to be changed.

(Students may want to make a group list of items from the story on the chalkboard. Then see how many additional electrical devices can be added to it.)

ENERGY

Current News

Skills:
Learning how electricity is produced

Materials:
Reproducible on page 26
Pencil

You already know that we depend on electricity in many, many ways every day. But do you know how electricity is produced? In this lesson we will learn one way in which electricity is made and then sent to your home. Your worksheet shows steps in the process, but they are not in order. Listen as I explain the process and number the pictures from 1 to 9 as I talk.

1. First, the sun's energy is absorbed in the leaves of plants living thousands of years ago. When they die, the plants are gradually buried deeper and deeper.

2. The plants are squeezed into coal by the weight of the earth and rock above them. People who work in coal mines extract the coal to be used.

3. Coal is delivered to power stations.

4. The coal is burned in a power station to boil water. This makes steam which turns turbines which operate generators. (You should now have four pictures numbered.)

5. Inside every generator is a magnet and a coil of wire. The turbines turn either the magnet or the coil of wire which produces electricity.

6. From the power station, the electrical current goes to a transformer, where the voltage (or pressure) is increased.

7. From the transformer, the current is sent out through a system of pylons, towers and wires to a meter in your home. (You should now have seven pictures labeled.)

8. From the meter in your home, the electricity goes through a circuit breaker or fuse box. This is a safety device which will break the flow of electricity if it becomes too strong.

9. Finally, the electricity flows through wires which end at sockets, where you can plug in an electrical appliance.

Double-check your work as I quickly read through the nine steps again. Then write your name in the top left corner of the page.

Note that power stations can run on fuels other than coal to produce electricity, including oil, natural gas, water power or nuclear energy.

Current News

Reproducible for use with page 25.

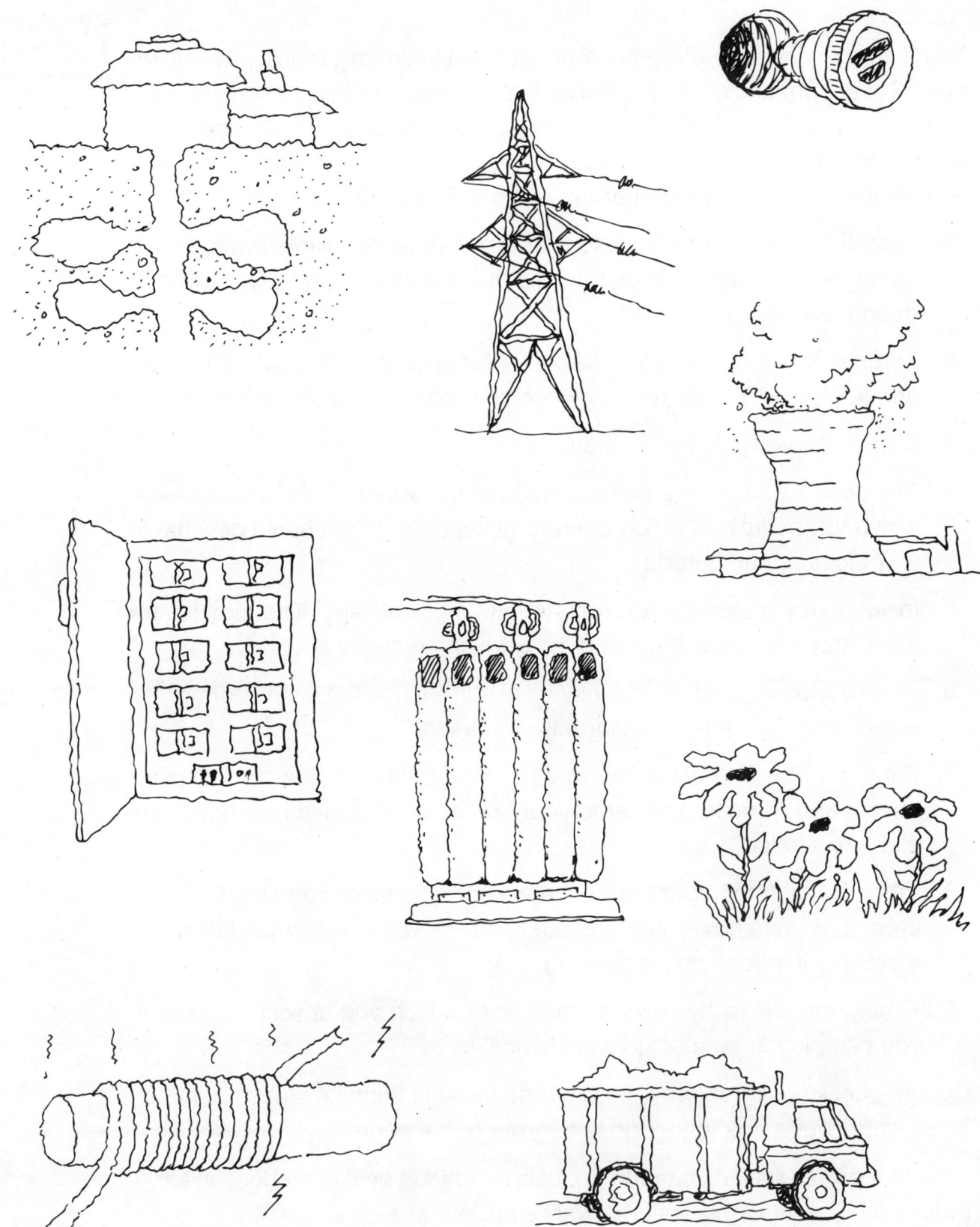

ENERGY

Get to Work!

Skills: Defining and giving examples of potential and kinetic energy

Materials: Lined paper, Pencil

In this lesson we will learn about energy and work. You should now number your paper from 1 to 15, and then listen for directions as we go through the lesson.

Energy is the ability to do work. When we speak of work in scientific terms, we mean that work is done when a force moves an object. You cannot see energy, but you can see what work it does. When you use your own energy to pedal a bike, you can see the bike move. You are doing work because you have moved the bike. Both you and the bike have kinetic energy. Electricity is kinetic motion because the current is caused by a huge number of moving electrons. The whirling beaters on a mixer have kinetic motion. List five more examples of kinetic energy by numbers 1 to 5 on your page.

Another kind of energy is potential energy. Objects at rest have potential energy if they have the ability to do work. A car sitting at the top of the hill has the ability to do work or to move. A swimmer ready to dive into the pool has potential energy. Now list five more examples of potential energy. Use lines 6 to 10 on your page.

Often objects change from having potential energy to having kinetic energy. For example, if you roll a bowling ball down a bowling lane, the 10 pins first have potential energy. When the ball hits them and knocks them around, those moving pins then have kinetic energy. List two more examples of objects at rest changing into objects in motion. Use numbers 11 and 12.

The reverse action is also possible. Moving objects can stop, and yet have the ability to do work. A moving car that brakes and stops at a railroad crossing is one example. List two more examples of objects with kinetic energy changing to having potential energy. Use numbers 13 and 14 on your page.

Write your name on line 15.

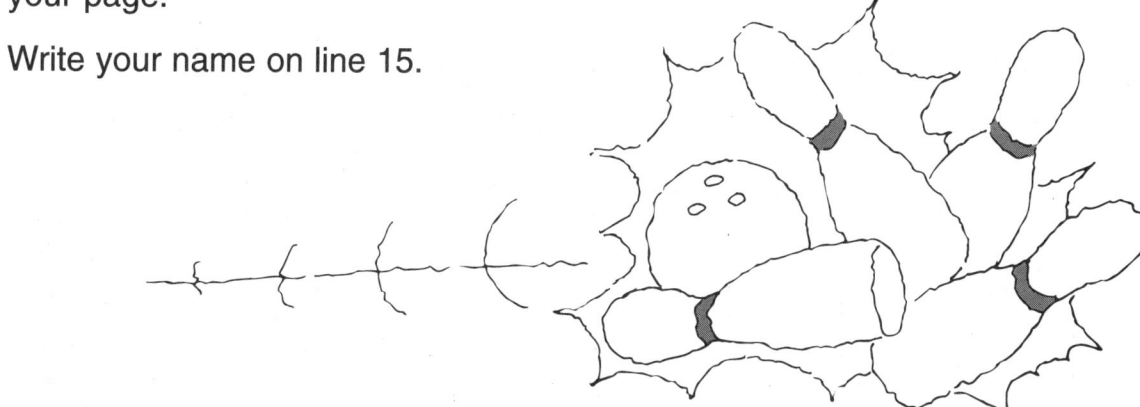

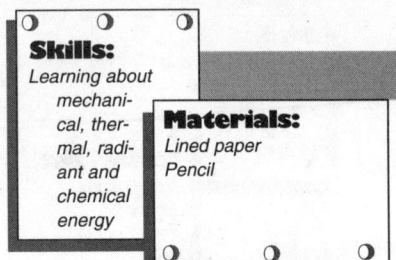

Skills: Learning about mechanical, thermal, radiant and chemical energy

Materials: Lined paper, Pencil

ENERGY

Four Forms

First write your name in the top right corner of the page. Number from 1 to 15.

There are several different types of kinetic and potential energy. In this lesson we will study four different forms of energy. I will list these on the board for your reference.

      Mechanical   Thermal   Radiant   Chemical

Mechanical energy is the energy of moving objects. A moving fan blade or the moving parts of an engine both have mechanical energy. They have the ability to do work. You use your own mechanical energy when you run. You use mechanical energy when you use a hammer to hit a nail.

Thermal energy that flows from an object is heat. The heat comes from the movement of the tiny particles that make up matter. All particles in an object have kinetic energy, but not every particle has the same amount of energy. We measure the amount of energy of the particles in an object by finding its temperature. If you poured hot coffee into a mug, the handle on the mug would become warm. The coffee has thermal energy that flows to the cup and handle.

Radiant energy is a form of energy that travels in waves. The best example is solar energy. It is radiant energy from the sun. It does work as it warms objects. It travels through empty space. Light is radiant energy which can also travel through empty space. It can travel through some kinds of matter, too, such as glass.

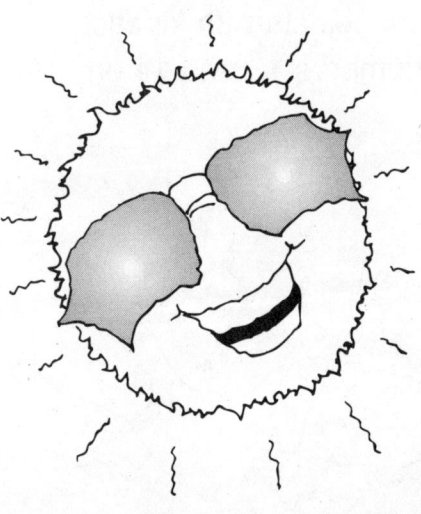

Chemical energy is stored in matter when atoms join together. It can be released when matter goes through a change. It converts to other forms of energy. For example, wood and other fuels contain chemical energy. When they are burned, the energy is released as heat and light. Another good example occurs right within your own body. When you eat, the chemical energy stored in foods releases to produce mechanical energy to help you move. It also produces thermal energy which warms you.

ENERGY

Four Forms

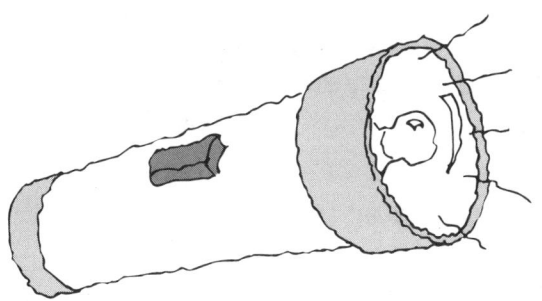

Now, let's see how well you've been listening. For numbers 1 to 8, I will describe one of these four types of energy. Write the first letter of the answer on your line. For example, if I describe thermal energy, write the letter T.

1. A gardener grows plants in a greenhouse.
2. A large bulldozer moves a pile of dirt.
3. A battery is used to power a flashlight.
4. A person takes a warm bath to get rid of chills.
5. Gasoline is burned to power a car.
6. Windmill blades turn to pump water out of the ground.
7. Solar panels are used to heat a home.
8. You eat a big meal before playing basketball.

For the next numbers, write the word *true* or *false* on each line.

9. Mechanical energy is the energy of moving objects.
10. Thermal energy that flows from an object is heat.
11. Your body releases radiant energy.
12. Light is a form of radiant energy.
13. Temperature is the measure of chemical energy.
14. Chemical energy is stored in matter when atoms join together.
15. Radiant energy travels through empty space.

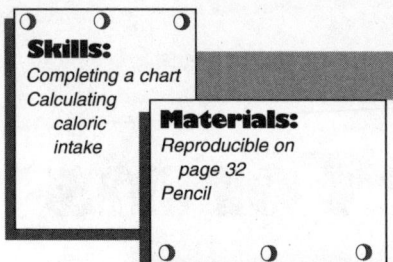

ENERGY

Counting Calories

You may already know that food contains chemical energy which your body changes into mechanical and thermal energy. The chemical energy in food is measured in units called calories. If you didn't take in enough calories, you would be low on energy. You would lose weight and eventually you would die. If you take in more calories than you use, the extra energy is stored in your body as fat. If too much extra energy is stored, you eventually gain weight.

Part 1

Now write your name in the top right corner of your worksheet. The chart on your page shows the amount of calories contained in some foods. You will notice that some of the information is missing. Listen carefully as I read you that information, and add it in the correct places on the chart.

Let's begin with *dairy products*. One cup of whole milk contains 150 calories. Add the number of calories to this line on your chart. Skim milk has 85 calories per cup. A chocolate milk shake has 300 calories in one cup, and one cup of cottage cheese contains about 215 calories.

Next, move on to the *meat, poultry and fish*. The roast beef has 160 calories. A three-ounce lean broiled pork chop has 270 calories. Three ounces of roasted white chicken has 140 calories. Frozen fish sticks that have been reheated have about 70 calories each.

Now let's do the foods containing *grains.* One plain bagel has 200 calories, and one slice of whole wheat bread has about 65 calories. One bran muffin has 140 calories. One cup of cooked oatmeal contains 145 calories. A one-ounce serving of corn cereal has 110 calories. A serving of 10 small pretzel sticks contains just 10 calories. A serving of four average chocolate chip cookies has about 180 calories.

Fruits and vegetables are next. One fresh apple contains about 80 calories, and one banana has 105 calories. One cup of orange juice has 110 calories. One cup of raisins contains 440 calories, and one cup of plain strawberries has about 45 calories. One cup of cooked green beans has 35 calories. One raw carrot has about 30 calories, and one stalk of celery has just 5 calories. One ear of cooked sweet corn has 85 calories. A peeled baked potato has 145 calories, and one cup of mashed potatoes yields 160 calories. For more calories, a cup of potato salad has 360 calories. Tomato soup contains about 160 calories per cup when made with milk.

Finally, one tablespoon of margarine has about 100 calories. One tablespoon of sugar has 45 calories, and one tablespoon of jam has 55 calories.

ENERGY

Counting Calories

(Teacher: This could be completed at a later time, if desired.)

Part 2

Now that your chart is complete, use the following information to find the total calories for two different meals. Stan and Dan are adult brothers. Stan is very thin and active and needs to gain some weight. In the box that says *Stan's Breakfast,* write down the number of calories in the foods that he eats for breakfast. His breakfast is one cup of whole milk, one cup of oatmeal, a half cup of raisins and one bagel with a tablespoon of margarine and a tablespoon of jam. Find the total calories in Stan's breakfast and circle it.

Next find the calories in Dan's breakfast, using the space on your page. Dan is not very active, and he is slightly overweight. He is trying to eat fewer calories. For breakfast Dan eats one cup of corn cereal, one cup of skim milk, one cup of orange juice and one piece of whole wheat bread toasted and spread with a tablespoon of jam. Find the total calories of his meal and circle it.

Notice that both men can have a balanced, nutritious breakfast even though they are each getting a different amount of calories.

Now write a menu for Stan's lunch in the box on your page. It could be his main meal for the day. Choose a variety of foods and include three or more fruits and vegetables. Make a reasonable combination of food that will total 1200 and 1500 calories. Find the total number of calories and circle it.

Finally, write a leaner menu for Dan. Again, choose a good variety of foods with three or more fruits and veggies. This time include only 600 to 900 calories. Find the total number of calories and circle it.

(Teacher: If time allows, have several students share their menus for Stan's and Dan's lunches. Evaluate them for balance and nutrition as well as calories. Save calorie charts for use with page 34, if desired.)

Counting Calories

Reproducible for use with pages 30 and 31.

Dairy Products

Food and Amount	Calories
whole milk, 1 cup	_____
skim milk, 1 cup	_____
_____, 1 cup	300
cottage cheese, 1 cup	_____

Meat, Poultry and Fish

Food and Amount	Calories
lean roast beef, 3 oz.	_____
_____, 3 oz.	270
roast chicken, 3 oz. white	_____
fish sticks, each one	_____

Grains

Food and Amount	Calories
plain bagel, one	_____
whole wheat bread, one slice	_____
_____, one	140
_____, 1 cup	145
corn cereal, 1 oz.	_____
pretzel sticks, _____	10
doughnut, one	220
chocolate chip cookies, ____	180

Fruits and Vegetables

Food and Amount	Calories
apple, one fresh	80
_____, one	105
orange juice, _____	110
raisins, 1 cup	_____
strawberries, 1 cup plain	_____
green beans, 1 cup cooked	_____
_____, one raw	_____
_____, one stalk	5
sweet corn, one ear	_____
baked potato, one peeled	_____
mashed potatoes, 1 cup	_____
_____, 1 cup	360
tomato soup, 1 cup	_____

Miscellaneous

Food and Amount	Calories
margarine, 1 T.	_____
sugar, 1 T.	_____
_____, 1 T.	55

Stan's Breakfast	Dan's Breakfast

Stan's Lunch	Dan's Lunch

ENERGY

Burning Up!

Skills: Finding number of calories used in different activities

Materials: Lined paper, Pencil

In the last lesson you learned about the number of calories you take into your body through the foods you eat. In this lesson you will learn about burning up those calories, or energy, through various activities. First write your name in the upper right corner of your page. Then number your paper from 1 to 10.

Write these activities on each numbered line in order as I read them to you, beginning with number 1: sleeping, reading, driving, housework, slow cycling, swimming, roller skating, tennis, basketball, running.

Now follow my directions to calculate the average number of calories a person might use while doing each of these activities for one hour. Write the number of calories next to each activity on the same line. Note that these are arranged from ones using the least to the greatest number. Also notice that these numbers are only approximations and will vary based on each person's weight and the speed of the exercise.

A. Sleeping burns 60 calories per hour.

B. Swimming uses five times as many calories per hour as does sleeping.

C. Tennis uses seven times the amount of calories as does sleeping.

D. Slow cycling on a bike burns half as many calories per hour as playing tennis.

E. A person reading burns 40 more calories per hour than a person who is asleep.

F. A basketball player burns five times more calories than the person who is sitting in the stands reading the newspaper.

G. Driving a car requires twice as much energy as sleeping.

H. Roller skating burns 50 more calories per hour than does swimming.

I. Doing housework burns 80 more calories per hour than does sitting and reading a book.

J. Running uses five times as much energy as doing normal housework.

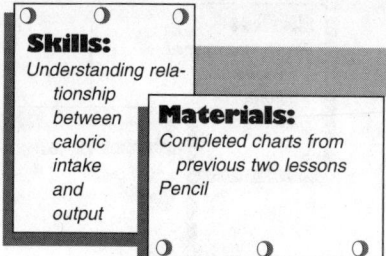

Skills: Understanding relationship between caloric intake and output

Materials: Completed charts from previous two lessons Pencil

ENERGY

In and Out

Use the food calorie chart and calorie burning chart from the previous lessons to answer the questions I will read you. Draw a line down the center of your page dividing it into two columns. Now draw four evenly spaced lines going across the page so that you have four rows with two boxes in each row. Number the boxes from 1 to 8 beginning with the top left box, then the top right box and so on.

For each number I will read you a problem that requires you to use the information on your two charts. Use the box as a work space. Circle your final answer.

1. In one 24-hour day, Dan spent 8 hours sleeping, 2 hours driving, 8 hours sitting at his desk, 1 hour swimming, 1 hour doing housework and 4 hours sitting reading and watching television. How many calories did he use in all?

2. Suppose in the same day that Dan ate 700 calories for breakfast, 800 calories for lunch, 1200 calories for dinner and 300 calories in snacks. Would Dan gain or lose weight for that day?

3. In one 24-hour day, Stan spent 8 hours sleeping, 8 hours reading at his desk, 2 hours doing housework, 1 hour driving, 2 hours playing basketball, 1 hour slow cycling and 2 hours reading and watching television. How many calories did Stan use that day?

4. Suppose in the same day that Stan ate 850 calories for breakfast, 900 calories for lunch, 1000 calories for dinner and 100 calories for snacks. Would Stan gain or lose weight for that day?

5. Jan wants to plan a nutritious lunch that contains about 800 calories. Plan two possible menus for her.

6. Now list two ways she could burn up those calories in an afternoon.

7. Estimate your activities for one Saturday afternoon. Find the number of calories you might use up. Then plan a lunch menu that will supply that number of calories.

8. Write your name and today's date in this box.

34

TLC10182 Copyright © Teaching & Learning Company, Carthage, IL 62321-0010

ENERGY

Renewability

Skills: Identifying renewable and nonrenewable energy sources

Materials: Lined paper, Pencil

The energy we use to run our homes, businesses, cars and machines comes from a variety of sources. Some of these sources are renewable; that is, they can be easily replaced and used again. The sun is an example of a renewable energy source. Much of our energy, however, comes from nonrenewable sources—ones that cannot be easily replaced. An example is coal which is made of fossilized plants that lived hundreds or thousands of years ago.

Number your paper from 1 to 13. Listen as I read an energy source for each number. Think about if it's renewable or not. Write R on the line if it is a renewable energy source. Write N if it is a nonrenewable source.

1. wind energy
2. petroleum
3. wood
4. solar cells
5. gasoline
6. kerosene
7. tidal energy
8. natural gas
9. geothermal energy
10. hydroelectric power
11. crude oil
12. nuclear power
13. Write your name on line 13.

Skills:
Following directions
Learning about the law of conservation of energy

Materials:
Reproducible on page 37
Pencil

ENERGY

Cross Out

You have already learned that energy can change forms. For example, the chemical energy in a flashlight battery changes to electric energy that heats a wire in a light bulb. The result is light. There is an important scientific fact related to this transfer of energy hidden in the boxes on your worksheet. Follow my directions to discover the fact. First write your name in the top right corner of your page.

1. In column B, cross out all words of five letters.
2. In row 4, cross out all the words of four syllables.
3. In column C, cross out all two-letter words.
4. In row 5 cross out every word that is a nonrenewable energy source.
5. Look anywhere in the chart to find three subjects you might have in school. Cross out all three.
6. In column F, cross out all words that rhyme with *care*.
7. In row 3, cross out the word that describes energy in motion.
8. In column D, cross out any word of less than six letters that ends in y.
9. Cross out every number word in the chart.
10. In row 6, cross out words that are used to name renewable energy sources.
11. In column A, cross out the word that comes last in alphabetical order.
12. Write the remaining words in the last lines at the bottom of the page. Go in order from left to right and top to bottom.

Cross Out

Reproducible for use with page 36.

	A	B	C	D	E	F
1	When	The	If	science	law	pair
2	of	major	conservation	carry	of	two
3	math	energy	says	kinetic	one	rare
4	that	impossible	to	energy	generator	cannot
5	coal	be	reading	today	created	oil
6	or	every	wind	destroyed	sun	there

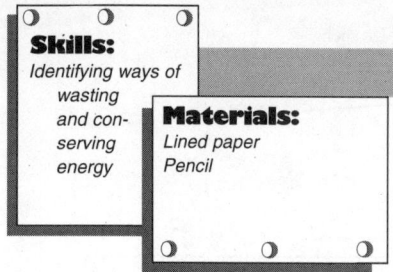

Skills: Identifying ways of wasting and conserving energy

Materials: Lined paper, Pencil

ENERGY

Save It!

We use a lot of energy to live and work. Much of the energy we use today is for heating and cooling buildings and for transporting people and goods. Many of the resources used for these activities are limited. They can be replaced when they are used up. That is why it is important to find ways to save our energy resources.

First write your name in the top right corner of your page. Then number from 1 to 15. For each number I will read an activity. If it is one that reduces energy use, draw a smiley face on that line. If it is an activity that uses extra energy, draw a frown.

1. drying clothes outside on a clothesline
2. bicycling to work or school
3. turning up the heat in your home in winter
4. using the regular oven instead of using the microwave for small amounts of food
5. riding a bus instead of driving a car
6. adding insulation to the walls and attic of a house
7. leaving the television on all day
8. baking several things in the oven at one time
9. running the dishwasher when it is half full
10. increasing the temperature in a hot water heater
11. switching from a large car to a smaller one
12. frequently opening and closing the refrigerator door
13. cooling a room by opening a window instead of using air conditioning
14. switching off lights when leaving the room
15. Write one way you can conserve energy on line 15.

PRE/POSTTEST FOR PART 3

Water

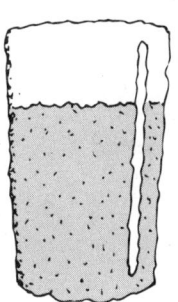

Materials:
Lined paper
Pencil

Write your name in the top right corner of your page.

1. List three direct uses of water in your everyday life.
2. Give two indirect uses of water.
3. Suppose that four people in your family each take four showers a week that last for 10 minutes each. If your shower uses six gallons of water per minute, how many gallons of water does your family use for showers in one week?

(Teacher: For numbers 4-6, write these words on the board: condensation, evaporation, precipitation, transpiration and infiltration.)

Use one of the words from the chalkboard to complete the sentences in numbers 4-6. Write just the word off the board on your paper.

4. Forms of water vapor that are heavy enough to fall to the Earth such as rain, snow and hail are called _____.
5. The changing of liquid water into water vapor is known as _____.
6. The process by which water vapor seeps into the soil is called _____.
7. Name one state in the USA that is landlocked.
8. Name one state in the USA that is not landlocked.
9. What is the name of a storm with strong, rotating winds? Hurricanes and tornadoes are both examples of this kind of storm. It is spelled with seven letters.
10. What do we call a large mass of ice and snow that moves slowly down a valley? It is spelled with seven letters.

(Teacher: For 11 and 12, write these words on the board: atom, nucleus, element, compound.)

Use one of these words from the chalkboard to complete the sentences in numbers 11 and 12. Write just the word off the board on your paper.

11. The word that refers to matter that is made of only one kind of atom is _____.
12. Matter made up of two or more elements is called a _____.
13. Name the two elements that make up water.

Skills:
Increase student awareness of our extensive water usage

Materials:
Paper
Pencil
Chalkboard

WATER

Water, Water, Everywhere

Divide the class into teams of four or five students each. Instruct each team to list as many ways as possible that we use water in our everyday lives. Allow several minutes for this. Encourage them to list direct, as well as indirect, uses. Then ask each group to share its list with the class. As each group shares, write a composite list for the entire classroom on the chalkboard. Have someone copy the composite list on a wall-size chart, allowing space for future additions.

Ask students to vote on which activities they think use the most/least water.

Ask students to estimate how much water they use directly in one day by themselves.

Ask students to estimate how much water their entire household uses in one day. Then have them multiply to figure out how many gallons they use in one week, one month and one year.

(Note: One study estimates the average American directly uses 87 gallons of water per day; other studies are higher. Some studies go as high as 300 gallons a day where lawn watering is more extensive. Indirect uses also account for high water usage. One study estimates that more than 4500 gallons are needed to produce three balanced meals a day for one person!)

Proceed directly to the next lesson, if desired, to do some actual calculations on water usage.

WATER

Water "Guess"timates

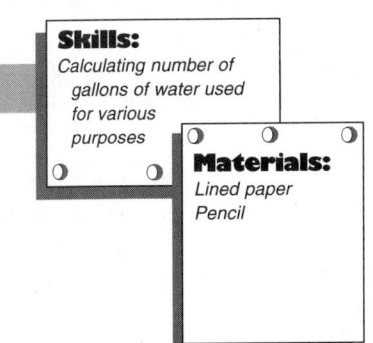

Skills:
Calculating number of gallons of water used for various purposes

Materials:
Lined paper
Pencil

(Teacher: If desired, send a note home with students before beginning this lesson, asking families to send back an estimate of these numbers for their household: showers per week, toilet flushes per day, loads of laundry per week, pounds of potatoes eaten per week and loaves of bread eaten per week.)

In this lesson we will estimate the number of gallons of water used in your homes for various purposes. To do this, first make a chart on your paper. You need to draw three vertical lines from top to bottom to divide your page into four columns. Then draw four horizontal lines dividing the paper into five rows. You should now have 20 boxes on your page.

Next we will label each row with a different use of water. In the left-hand corner write these words, one per box, from top to bottom: *shower, toilet, washing machine, potatoes and bread.*

Now go back to the first row. Estimate how many showers people in your home take during a normal week. Then guess about how many minutes each shower lasts. Write these two numbers in the second box. Then multiply them together to determine how many minutes in all the shower is running in your home during one week. Write the answer, label it in minutes and circle it. In the third box, write *8 gallons*. This is the amount of water used per minute in an average shower. In the final box on the first row, multiply your answer from the second box by the number in the third box. Find the answer, label it *gallons of water used in the shower per week* and underline it.

We'll follow a similar pattern for the remaining three rows.

Row 2

Guess how many times the toilet is flushed in your home in a day and write it in the second box. Then multiply this by 7 to find how many times it is flushed per week. Circle this number. In the third box, write *6 gallons*. This is the amount of water used per flush in an ordinary non "low-flow" toilet. In the last box, multiply the numbers from the second and third boxes. Write the answer, label it *gallons of water used in the toilet per week* and underline it.

TLC10182 Copyright © Teaching & Learning Company, Carthage, IL 62321-0010

Water "Guess"timates

Row 3

Try to figure out how many washer loads of laundry are done in your home in one week. Write this number in the second box. In the third box write *20 gallons*, the amount of water used per load. In the last box, multiply the numbers from the second and third boxes. Write the answer, label it *gallons used in the washer per week* and underline it.

Rows 4 and 5 deal with less obvious, indirect uses of water. For example, someone calculated the water needed to produce one egg. Including the amount of water used to raise grain to feed the chicken, the total water needed came to a surprising 120 gallons!

Row 4

Estimate the pounds of potatoes (including potato products such as instant dehydrated potatoes, French fries, etc.) that your family eats in one week. Write this "guess"timate in the second box. In the third box write *23 gallons*, the number of gallons that were estimated to be used in growing one pound of potatoes. In the last box, multiply the numbers from the second and third boxes. Write the answer, label it *gallons of water used to grow one week's worth of potatoes* and underline it.

Row 5

For the last row, estimate the number of loaves of bread your family consumes in one week. Write the number in the second box. In the third box, write *150 gallons,* the number of gallons needed to grow the grains used to make one loaf of bread. In the last box, multiply the numbers from the second and third boxes. Write the answer, label it *gallons of water used for one week's worth of bread* and underline it. Write your name at the bottom of this page.

Compare and discuss outcomes among different students.

WATER

The Water Cycle

Skills: Learning how water is used over and over in nature

Materials: Reproducible on page 44
Pencil

Water is constantly circulating and being used and reused in nature. The amount of water on the Earth always remains about the same, but it can follow many different routes and change into a variety of forms. We will look at these together as you study the worksheet in front of you. Write your name in the top right corner of the page. Notice that there are several blanks. You will need to listen to my instructions to complete each blank with the correct word. *(Note: You may wish to write the italicized words on the chalkboard first so that students may refer to them during the lesson.)*

First, write the word *ocean* in the blank to label the large body of water. About seven-eighths of the Earth's precipitation falls directly into the oceans.

Water from the ocean is warmed by the sun and evaporates into the atmosphere as water vapor. Write the word *evaporation* in the blank that shows this.

At higher altitudes, the air temperature is lower. The water vapor then condenses and forms a cloud. Write the word *condensation* in the blank in the cloud.

When enough water collects, it falls back to the Earth as rain, snow, sleet or hail. These are all forms of precipitation. Write the word *precipitation* in the blank that shows this part of the water cycle.

On the land, this precipitation can go in several directions. First, it can land on the ground and immediately run off surfaces into lakes and rivers. This usually happens when the ground is rocky or very hard. Write the word *run-off* in the blank that shows this.

The rainwater can also infiltrate into the soil or be absorbed by plants. Write the word *infiltration* in the correct blank.

Finally, the water not absorbed by plants can become groundwater which eventually ends up back in springs, rivers and oceans. Write the word *groundwater* in the part of the picture that shows this.

Plants also release small amounts of water as it evaporates from their leaves. This process is called transpiration. Write the word *transpiration* in the correct place on your page.

The water cycle is an endless process. More water evaporates from ocean surfaces and plants, condenses to form clouds and falls back to Earth. Weather, climate and geographic features affect the rate and amounts of water that circulate between ocean, sky and land.

TLC10182 Copyright © Teaching & Learning Company, Carthage, IL 62321-0010

The Water Cycle

Reproducible for use with page 43.

Skills:
Map reading
Using a mileage scale

Materials:
Reproducible on page 46
Pencil
Colored pencils
Ruler
North America map

WATER

River Route

Write your name in the top right corner of your page. This map shows major rivers and lakes of the United States. These waterways have been very important to the growth of businesses and cities in the U.S. You will shade in parts of the map during this lesson. Remember to color lightly with your pencils so that you are able to read and write the words on the map.

First, study your classroom map to see what parts of the United States are bordered by water and what parts are bordered by land. Leave the United States blank, but color the land around it brown. Color the water, including the lakes that are shown, with a blue pencil.

A state is said to be *landlocked* if it is completely surrounded by land and does not border a lake or ocean. Can you recognize the state of Oklahoma on your map? This is one example of a landlocked state. Color all the landlocked states lightly with a red pencil. Color the states that border on water with a light yellow pencil. Count to see if there are more landlocked states or more that border on water. *(Note: The class may want to discuss together how they should color the state of Utah. Unlike the Great Lakes, the Great Salt Lake is completely inside the state, so Utah doesn't actually share a border with the water. Most will probably agree it should be colored red.)*

Next, plan a water trip. Use your classroom map to find six major U.S. cities that are located on major rivers or lakes. Add these cities to your map. Number them from 1 to 6, in the order in which you plan to visit them. With a ruler, draw a straight line to connect the cities in order. Use the mileage scale to calculate the approximate distance of your trip. Write the total mileage of your trip underneath your name.

Optional Activities for Older Students

Estimate a reasonable average driving speed. Then calculate how long it would take to drive across the route from beginning to end.

Estimate how many miles a car might travel on one gallon of gasoline. How many gallons would be needed to make this trip? At the current cost of gasoline, how much would you expect to pay for enough fuel to make the trip?

River Route

Reproducible for use with page 45.

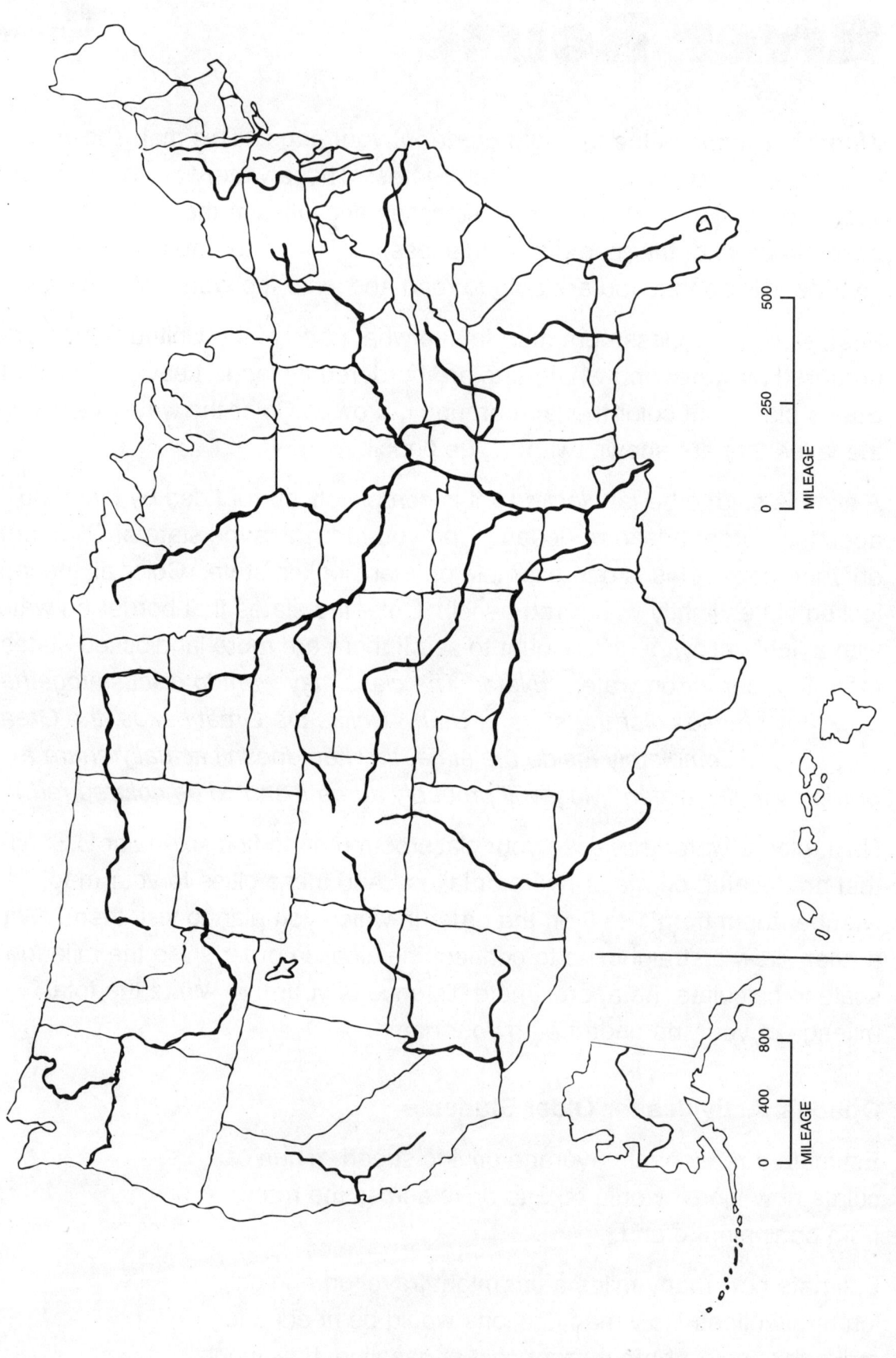

46

WATER

Precipitation Puzzler

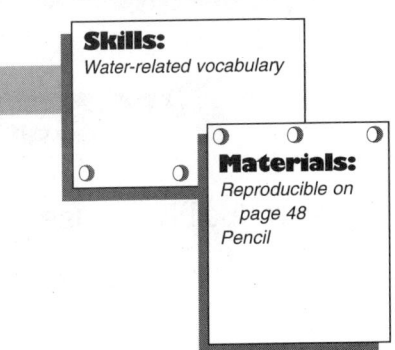

Skills:
Water-related vocabulary

Materials:
Reproducible on page 48
Pencil

When water falls to the Earth, it can be in the form of rain, snow, sleet or hail. In the morning you may see fog, mist, dew or frost. These are all forms of precipitation. Write the letters in PRECIPITATION in the circle blanks on your puzzle sheet. Write the P in the circled blank in the first line, the R in the circle blank on the second line and so on. These letters will be clues to help you complete the puzzle. Write your name in the top right corner of your page.

For each number, I will read you a clue. You need to think of the word I am describing and write it in the blanks, with one letter in each blank.

1. the degree of hotness or coldness of water
2. a storm with strong winds, low temperatures and lots of snow
3. a large mass of ice and snow that moves slowly down a valley
4. a storm with strong, rotating winds; hurricanes and tornadoes are both examples
5. frozen raindrops that often fall during thunderstorms
6. a violent tropical cyclone that starts in the Pacific Ocean
7. a rain that comes in fine, misty drops
8. partly frozen rain
9. water falling as drops
10. the sound made when lightning suddenly heats air, causing it to expand
11. a series of high, fast waves caused by earthquakes
12. an overflow of water in a place that is normally dry
13. frozen bits of water vapor that fall to the Earth as white flakes

Precipitation Puzzler

Reproducible for use with page 47.

1. ___ ___ ___ ◯ ___ ___ ___ ___ ___
2. ___ ___ ___ ___ ___ ◯ ___ ___ ___
3. ___ ___ ___ ___ ◯ ___ ___ ___
4. ___ ___ ___ ◯ ___ ___ ___ ___
5. ___ ___ ___ ◯ ___ ___ ___
6. ___ ___ ___ ◯ ___ ___ ___
7. ___ ___ ___ ◯ ___ ___ ___
8. ___ ___ ___ ___ ◯ ___ ___
9. ___ ___ ___ ◯ ___ ___
10. ___ ___ ___ ◯ ___ ___ ___ ___
11. ___ ___ ___ ◯ ___ ___ ___ ___ ___
12. ___ ___ ◯ ___ ___
13. ___ ___ ◯ ___ ___

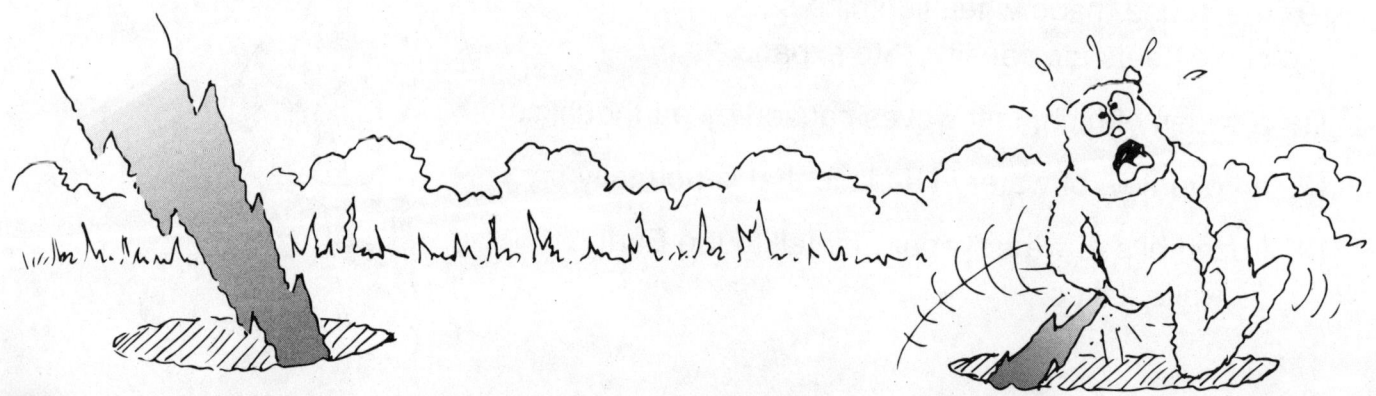

WATER

Compound Matchup

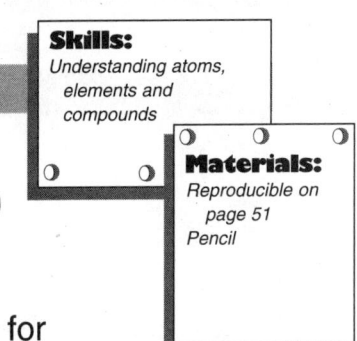

Skills: Understanding atoms, elements and compounds

Materials: Reproducible on page 51, Pencil

The chemical symbol for water is H_2O. This means that the smallest possible amount of water that can exist is made up of two parts of hydrogen and one part of oxygen.

Now let's back up and cover some key scientific terms as I go through a more detailed explanation. As I talk, read through the terms and definitions on your worksheet. Draw a line from each word to its correct meaning. You will have to use one definition twice.

(Note: Terms that appear on the student page are italicized here for your emphasis.)

If you look around, you will see many different types of matter. Each kind of matter has its own properties or characteristics. For example, water is a liquid that easily changes shape. A rock is very hard, and air is invisible.

Now think of the smallest things you know, such as a grain of sand or a speck of dust. Under a special microscope it is sometimes possible to see even the smaller units called atoms. An *atom* is the smallest piece of an element that has the properties of that element. For example, one atom of gold is the smallest amount of matter that has all the characteristics of gold. You would not be able to see it with your eye, however. All atoms have a central core called a *nucleus*, made up of *protons* and *neutrons*. *Electrons* surround the nucleus of the atom.

Matter that is made of only one kind of atom is an *element*. *Hydrogen*, *oxygen*, gold, copper and aluminum are all elements. There are more than 100 elements known to scientists, and each one is different because it has different atoms from all the rest. Each element is known by a symbol which is like an abbreviation for its name. H is the symbol for hydrogen, O is for oxygen, Au is for gold, Cu is for copper and Al is for aluminum. All elements are grouped as either metals or nonmetals. Some elements, like hydrogen and oxygen, are gases, and they are nonmetals.

TLC10182 Copyright © Teaching & Learning Company, Carthage, IL 62321-0010

WATER
Compound Matchup

Most materials on Earth are not elements. Remember that elements are made of only one kind of atom, and there are a limited number of them. Yet there are millions of different kinds of substances on the Earth. That is because many materials are *compounds*, matter made of atoms of two or more elements. In compounds the elements are combined chemically and cannot be separated easily.

Sugar is a compound formed in water from the elements carbon, hydrogen and oxygen.

Rust is a compound formed when oxygen in air or water combines with iron.
Water, as we've already stated, is a compound formed from hydrogen and oxygen.

It is strange to realize that hydrogen and oxygen are both colorless gases. They have no smell or taste. Hydrogen will burn very quickly in oxygen. Yet when these elements are combined chemically, they form water, which we can see and even drink!

Now read over the terms and definitions on your page again to see if you've matched them correctly. Write your name at the bottom of the page.

Optional Follow-Up

Introduce students to the Periodic Table of Elements. Challenge them to learn 10 to 20 element names, characteristics and symbols.

Compound Matchup

Reproducible for use with pages 49 and 50.

1. atom
2. nucleus
3. protons, neutrons and electrons
4. element
5. compound
6. hydrogen
7. oxygen
8. sugar
9. rust
10. water

A. matter that is made of only one kind of atom
B. a compound containing hydrogen and oxygen atoms
C. a compound formed from oxygen and iron
D. parts of an atom
E. the smallest part of an element that has the properties of the element
F. a compound made of carbon, hydrogen and oxygen
G. the central core of an atom
H. an element that makes up water
I. matter made of two or or elements

Materials:
Reproducible on page 53
Pencil

PRE/POSTTEST FOR PART 4

Animals

Write your name in the top right corner of your page. Write today's date underneath it.

1. You should find the words *vertebrates* and *invertebrates* on the first line of your paper. I will list five animals. Write the name of each one under the correct column to show whether it is a vertebrate or an invertebrate. The animals are: cat, trout, crab, bee, toad.

For the next three blanks, you will see five groups of animals on your page. I will read you a description of one or more of these groups. Write just the first letter of the group or groups that I am describing for each number.

2. These are warm-blooded animals.
3. These animals have backbones.
4. These live part of their lives in water and part on land.

For the next two lines, I will read you some clues. Figure out the key words and write them in the first blanks. Then take the correct part of each key word to form the name of a common mammal.

5. One third of an automobile plus two thirds of a bird that is active at night
6. Three fourths of a light that sits on a table plus one fourth of an object used in many sports

For number 7, listen to lengths of these four animals. Write the name of the longest one in the blank on the left side of the graph. Make a bar on the graph to show its length. Here are four animals and their lengths: The average bison is 12 feet long, a hippo is 13 feet long, a tapeworm is 33 feet long and an elephant is 24 feet long.

For numbers 8 and 9, write the scrambled letters I will read you in the first blank. Then unscramble them and write the name of an animal in the second blank. In the third blank, tell whether the animal is an insect, amphibian, reptile, bird or mammal.

8. mossoup
9. flurglob

For 10 and 11, I will read a statement. Write *F* if it is a fact and *O* if it is an opinion.

10. A young cow is called a heifer.
11. A young eel should be called an "eeling" rather than an "elver."

For 12 and 13, read the three statements at the bottom of your page. Then listen to the two statements I read. Write either *true* or *false* for each one.

12. Periwinkles have no backbones.
13. The black abalone is an invertebrate.

PRE/POSTTEST FOR PART 4
Animals

1. Vertebrates   Invertebrates

      Fish   Amphibians   Birds   Mammals   Reptiles

2. _____   3. _____   4. _____

5. Key words: _____, _____; Mammal: _____

6. Key words: _____, _____; Mammal: _____

7.

_____
Animal

0   5   10   15   20   25   30   35   40

Approximate Length in Feet

8. _____   _____   _____

9. _____   _____   _____

10. _____

11. _____

12. _____   13. _____

All mollusks are invertebrates.

Snails, mussels and periwinkles are mollusks.

All abalone are mollusks.

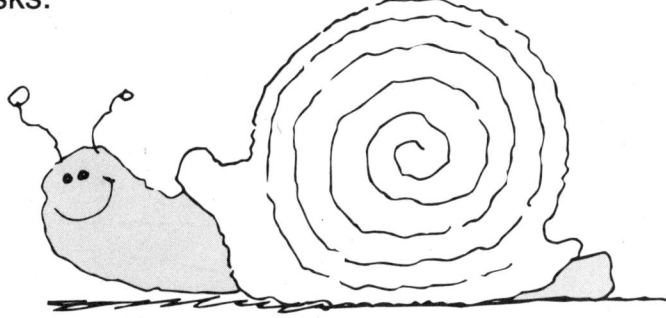

53

TLC10182 Copyright © Teaching & Learning Company, Carthage, IL 62321-0010

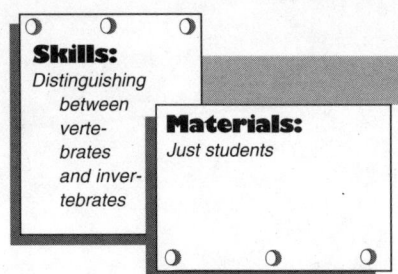

Skills: Distinguishing between vertebrates and invertebrates

Materials: Just students

ANIMALS

No Bones About It!

Use as a warm-up for Part 4.

Animals are classified as vertebrates or invertebrates based on whether or not the animals have backbones. Vertebrates are further placed into groups such as fish, birds, mammals and reptiles. Invertebrates are placed in groups based on their body structures. They range from very simple organisms such as sponges and jellyfish to more complex ones like starfish and insects.

Now listen as I call out the name of an animal. If the animal is a vertebrate (if it has a backbone), hold your arm up stiff and straight. If the animal is not a vertebrate (if it doesn't have a backbone), let your arm flop down to your side.

1. cat
2. octopus
3. kangaroo
4. lobster
5. flatworm
6. chicken
7. lizard
8. crab
9. snail
10. toad
11. trout
12. shrimp
13. bee
14. alligator
15. spider
16. coyote
17. roundworm
18. shark
19. snake
20. centipede

54   TLC10182 Copyright © Teaching & Learning Company, Carthage, IL 62321-0010

ANIMALS

Five Fits

Skills: Identifying features of different animal classifications

Materials: Lined paper, Pencil

There are five main groups of vertebrates, or animals with backbones. Those five groups are fish, amphibians, reptiles, birds and mammals. *(Teacher: Write the five groups on the chalkboard.)*

Number your paper from 1 to 12. For each number I will read a statement. You must decide which group or groups it describes. Write the first letter of each group that fits the description on the line.

Let's do the first one together. For number one, the statement is *These are cold-blooded animals.* Look over the five animal groups. You may know that fish, amphibians and reptiles are cold-blooded, so you would write F, A and R on your first line. Now let's continue.

2. These animals have body coverings of fur or hair.
3. These have scaly skins, gills and live in water.
4. These are warm-blooded animals.
5. These animals have backbones.
6. These live part of their lives in water and part on land.
7. These are covered with feathers and have strong, light skeletons.
8. These females produce milk to feed their young.
9. These are the most complex group of all animals.
10. Most animals in these groups lay eggs.
11. Most animals in these groups have a constant body temperature.
12. The group to which humans belong.

Write your name at the bottom of the page.

TLC10182 Copyright © Teaching & Learning Company, Carthage, IL 62321-0010

55

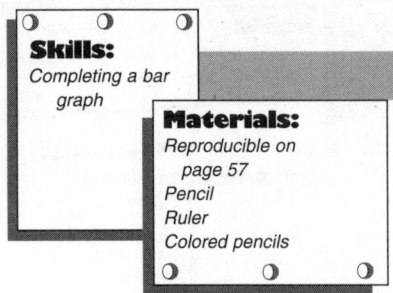

Skills: Completing a bar graph

Materials:
Reproducible on page 57
Pencil
Ruler
Colored pencils

ANIMALS

A Long Time

Use the graph on your worksheet to record the lengths of the 10 longest land animals in the world. I will supply the list of animals and the length of each one. You will need to write the name of each animal in the blank along the left edge of your graph. Then you should draw a horizontal bar for each animal. Use your ruler to make straight lines. Each bar needs to be drawn across the graph to show the length of the animal. Notice the vertical lines are labeled in feet at the bottom of the graph. Use colored pencils, if you like, to color the bars on your graph.

Here are the animals listed in alphabetical order. Starting with the top blank, write them down the left side of your graph: African elephant, American bison, Arabian camel, crocodile, giraffe, hippopotamus, royal python, Siberian tiger, tapeworm and white rhinoceros. *(Note: You may wish to help students with spelling and/or allow them to shorten the names of the animals.)*

Which of these animals do you think is the longest? Put a check mark by your prediction. Which do you think is the shortest of these long animals? Put an X by your choice.

Next draw the bars going across the graph. Here are the numbers you need:

African elephant–24 feet
American bison–13 feet
Arabian camel–12 feet
Crocodile–19 feet
Giraffe–19 feet

Hippopotamus–13 feet
Royal python–35 feet
Siberian tiger–11 feet
Tapeworm–33 feet
White rhinoceros–14 feet

Check your predictions. Were you correct?

Write a title for your graph. Write your name in the top left corner.

A Long Time

Reproducible for use with page 56.

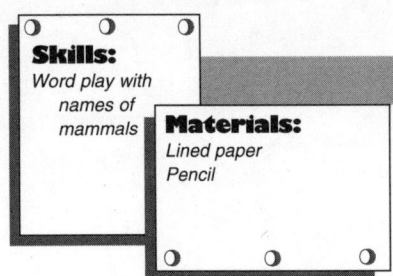

ANIMALS

Fractured Mammals

Number from 1 to 10, skipping a line between numbers. Write your name in the top right corner. In this lesson you need to decode the name of some common mammals. I will give you a fraction and a clue for a key word. When you have figured out the key word, write it down and then underline the correct fractional part of it. Finally, put the fractional parts of the key words together. The fractional parts will always be from the beginning of the word. Write the completed animal word on your paper. *(Note: 1/2 could mean 1 out of 2 letters, 2 out of 4 letters, 3 out of 6 and so on.)*

We'll do one example together.

1. 2/5 of a common, crisp fruit + 1/3 of a hearing organ
   The first key word is APPLE. The first 2/5 of it is AP.
   The second word is EAR. The first 1/3 of it is E.
   By putting those two parts together, you spell APE.

Now continue with the rest.

2. 1/3 of the color of the sky + 2/5 of the uppermost level of a house

3. 4/5 of a flat piece of fabric used on a bed + 1/3 of another word for hog

4. 2/5 of the opposite of black + 2/3 of everything + 1/3 of what baby birds hatch from

5. 2/3 of a piece of downhill snow sporting equipment + 2/5 of your dad's brother + 1/4 of the queen's husband

6. 1/2 of a precious metal + 2/3 of the past tense of *eat*

7. 2/5 of a sandy shore + 2/3 of a huge boat

8. 3/7 of the line where the sky seems to meet the Earth + 1/3 of a teeter-totter

9. 3/5 of a student + 2/7 of one of the structures built by ancient Egyptians

10. 3/5 of another word for cash + 1/2 of another word for save + 1/3 of the opposite of *no*

ANIMALS

Places, Please!

Skills: Unscrambling and classifying animal names

Materials: Reproducible on page 60. Pencil

Write your name in the top left corner of your page. Write today's date underneath.

Notice the numbered blanks on your page. For each one I will read a set of letters. You need to copy the letters just as I read them. Then try to unscramble the animal name and write it correctly under the correct column.

Let's do the first one together. Write the letters g, h, o in the blank. What does it spell? Yes, it's the word *hog*. Where should you write it? Yes, it goes under *Mammal*. Now continue with the rest.

2. broin
3. tabcob
4. fetyblurt
5. noflac
6. mossoup
7. osetrito
8. meanslarad
9. cikcter
10. everba
11. reffily
12. auaing
13. flurglob
14. rowrasp
15. gireaw

(Teacher: If students get "stuck," you may wish to supply the first letter.)

TLC10182 Copyright © Teaching & Learning Company, Carthage, IL 62321-0010

Places, Please!

Reproducible for use with page 59.

	Mammal	Amphibian	Reptile	Bird	Insect
1. _____	_____	_____	_____	_____	_____
2. _____	_____	_____	_____	_____	_____
3. _____	_____	_____	_____	_____	_____
4. _____	_____	_____	_____	_____	_____
5. _____	_____	_____	_____	_____	_____
6. _____	_____	_____	_____	_____	_____
7. _____	_____	_____	_____	_____	_____
8. _____	_____	_____	_____	_____	_____
9. _____	_____	_____	_____	_____	_____
10. _____	_____	_____	_____	_____	_____
11. _____	_____	_____	_____	_____	_____
12. _____	_____	_____	_____	_____	_____
13. _____	_____	_____	_____	_____	_____
14. _____	_____	_____	_____	_____	_____
15. _____	_____	_____	_____	_____	_____

ANIMALS

Group Troop

Skills:
Learning animal group terminology
Drawing

Materials:
Blank paper
Pencil

Animals often live together in groups, and these groups often have interesting names. For example, you may already know that fish travel in *schools*, and that wolves go in *packs*. Now see if you can learn some more group names as we work through this lesson.

First write your name in the top right corner of your page. Then divide your paper in half, both vertically and horizontally, so that you have four sections on your paper. I will read you a list of animals and their group names. You need to choose four to illustrate. Write your choices on your page, one in each section. Then draw sketches to show the double meaning of the group name. For example, for a school of fish, you could draw some fish in a classroom with a teacher, desks and books.

Listen now while I read this list, and make your four selections.

1. a cloud of gnats
2. a trip of goats
3. a bed of clams or oysters
4. a band of gorillas
5. a troop of kangaroos
6. a litter of pigs or kittens
7. a string of ponies
8. a pod of seals or whales
9. a knot of toads
10. a pride of lions
11. a bale of turtles

(Read the list two or three times and allow time for drawings.)

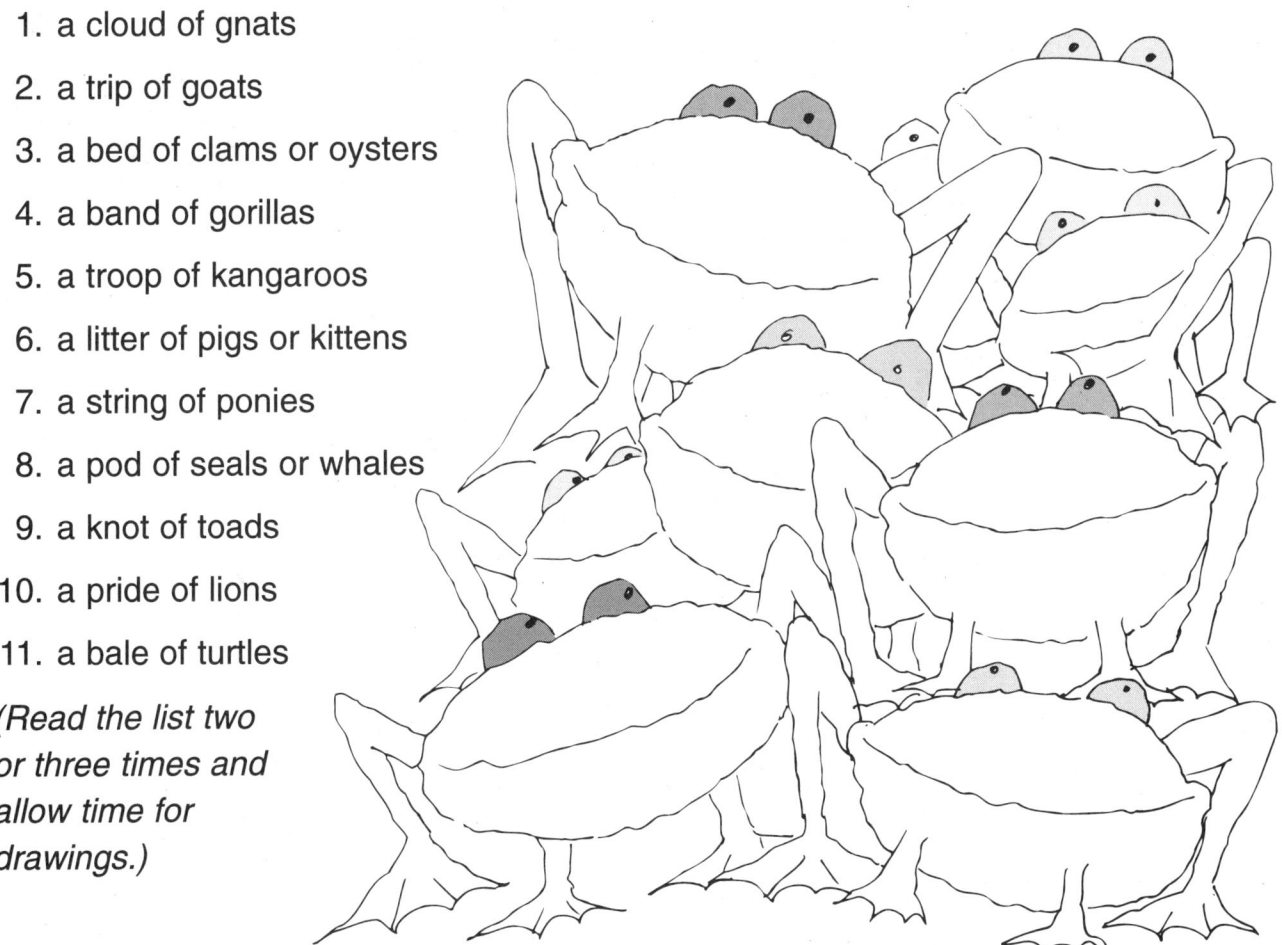

Skills:
Distinguishing between facts and opinion
Animal trivia

Materials:
Lined paper
Pencil

ANIMALS

Find the Facts

Write your name in the top right corner of your page. Number your paper from 1 to 15. For each number I will read a statement. If it is a fact, write F by the number. If it is someone's opinion, write O by the number. Remember, a fact is something that can be proven to be either true or false.

1. A young cow is called a heifer.
2. A young eel should be called an "eeling" rather than an "elver."
3. The best name for a group of geese is flock.
4. The average length of a guinea pig's life is four years.
5. The longest known life for a guinea pig was eight years.
6. The average grizzly bear lives for 25 years.
7. The ideal age for a pig is age 5.
8. A female whale is called a cow.
9. A male swan is called a cob.
10. A lion should be able to run faster than a zebra.
11. One of the slowest moving animals is the garden snail.
12. The sloth is the laziest animal.
13. The most popular house pet is a kitten.
14. The San Diego Zoo is the best zoo in the United States.
15. A chicken can run at a speed of nine miles per hour.

ANIMALS

Logic Lines

Skills:
Logic
Animal classification

Materials:
Reproducible on page 64
Pencil

Write your name in the top right corner of your worksheet. Notice that there are three sets of statements. You need to read each of the statements carefully, and then listen to the lines that I read you. If the line is true, write *true* in the numbered blank. If the line I read is false based on the statements printed on your sheet, write the word *false* in the numbered blank.

Set A: Read the four sentences on your worksheet. Then listen to these statements. Write *true* or *false* in the blanks.

1. Periwinkles have no backbones.
2. The black abalone is an invertebrate.
3. Snails are vertebrates.
4. A herring is an abalone.

Set B: Follow the same directions.

5. Butterflies are invertebrates.
6. Spiders are insects.
7. Butterflies are arachnids.
8. Monarch butterflies are insects.

Set C: Follow the same directions.

9. A stargazer has a three-chamber heart.
10. A grebe is not a fish.
11. A stargazer has gills.
12. A stargazer is a vertebrate.

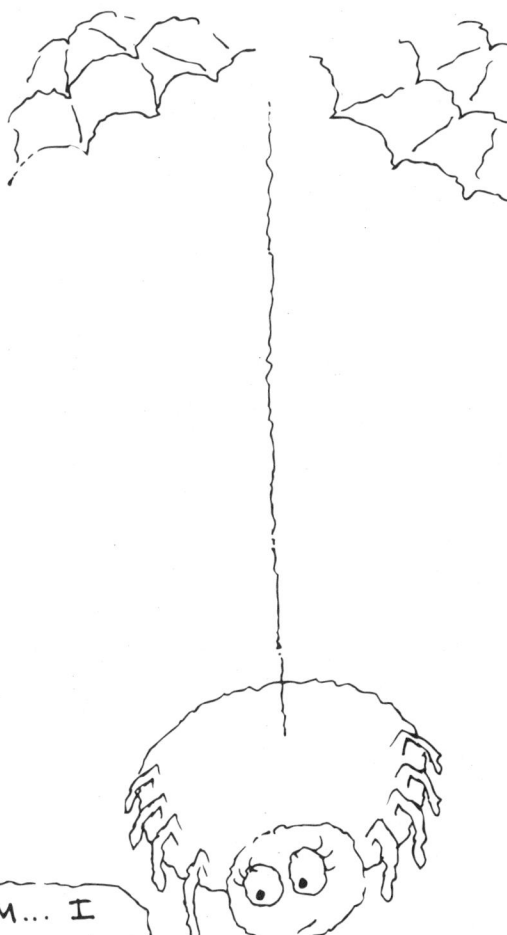

HEY, MOM... I JUST FRIGHTENED SOME LITTLE GIRL WHO WAS EATING CURDS AND WHEY.

Logic Lines

Reproducible for use with page 63.

Set A
All mollusks are invertebrates.
Snails, mussels and periwinkles are mollusks.
All abalones are mollusks.
Herrings are not mollusks.

1. _____ 2. _____ 3. _____ 4. _____

Set B
All insects and arachnids are invertebrates.
Insects have six legs; arachnids have eight legs.
All butterflies are insects.
All spiders are arachnids.

5. _____ 6. _____ 7. _____ 8. _____

Set C
All fish have gills and backbones.
All fish have hearts with two chambers.
A stargazer is a fish.
A grebe does not have fins.

9. _____ 10. _____ 11. _____ 12. _____

PRE/POSTTEST FOR PART 5

Materials:
Reproducible on page 66
Pencil

The Human Body

Write your name in the top right corner of your page.

For the first two blanks, write the word *true* or *false* for these statements:

1. People are taller in the morning than they are in the evening.
2. Your brain weighs less than one pound.
3. Put the names of these bones in the correct blanks by the skeleton: patella, tibia, femur, phalanges. You will have two extra blanks.

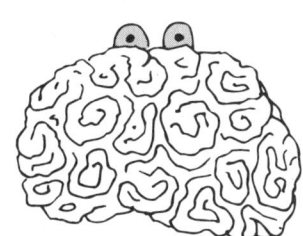

4. Label these parts of the heart: left ventricle, right atrium.
5.-6. Supply the missing letters to spell the names of two bones.
7. Circle the parts of the body that are used to help you taste food.

For 8 and 9, write the correct answer.

8. What are the big vessels that take blood into your heart called?

    A. pumps   B. arteries   C. veins

9. In what part of your body does the blood pick up its fresh supply of oxygen?

    A. brain   B. stomach   C. lungs

10. Howard's heart beats 16 times in 10 seconds. What is his heart rate per minute?

In numbers 11 and 12, find two organs of the body whose names have been intertwined. The order of the letters has not been changed. Write the organs in the blanks underneath. In the third blank, write the name of the body system to which both belong.

For 13 and 14, I will read a set of four words. Find the word in each set that does not belong. Write it in the blank.

13. tendon, ligament, cartilage, brain
14. trachea, lung, liver, diaphragm

65

PRE/POSTTEST FOR PART 5
The Human Body

1. _____
2. _____

3. a. _____
   b. _____
   c. _____
   d. _____
   e. _____
   f. _____

4.

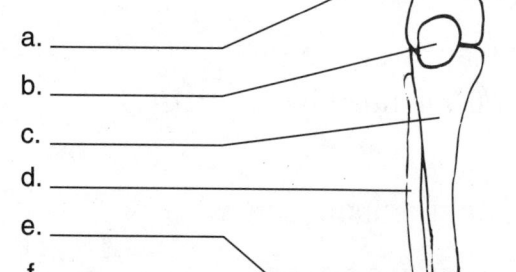
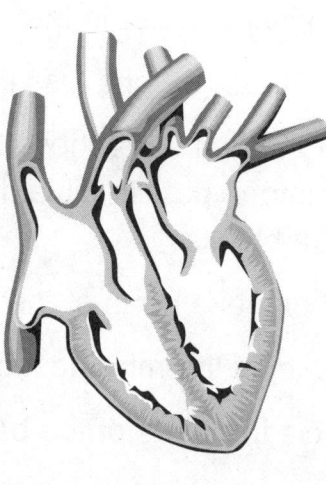

5. F E _ _ _
6. _ _ N D _ B _ _
7. nerves   taste buds   pupil   brain   tongue   hammer
8. _____
9. _____
10. _____
11. S L I T O V E M A R C H
    _____, _____; _____
12. A V E O R I T A N
    _____, _____; _____
13. _____
14. _____

THE HUMAN BODY

Trivial True and False

Skills: Learning trivia about the human body

Materials: Just students

Use as a warm-up for Part 5.

I will read several statements about the human body. If you think the statement is true, stand up. If you think it is false, sit down. We will discuss the statements as we go.

(Teacher: See answer key for explanations.)

1. Bones are the hardest material in your body.
2. You have more bones as a baby than you do as an adult.
3. The human skull is one large bone.
4. Children usually have a total of 20 "baby" teeth.
5. The tongue is the only organ needed to taste food.
6. People are taller in the morning than in the evening.
7. Electric signals travel along nerves at a speed of 300 miles per hour.
8. Your brain weighs less than a pound.
9. Your ribs all connect to the breastbone, or sternum, which is in the center of your chest.
10. When you sneeze, you can blow air at hurricane force.
11. Blood cells are made inside some of your bones.
12. There is no such thing as a double-jointed person.

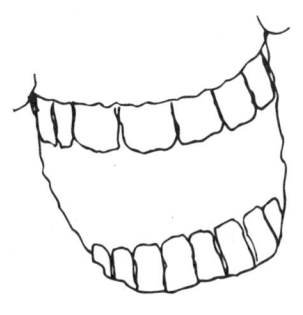

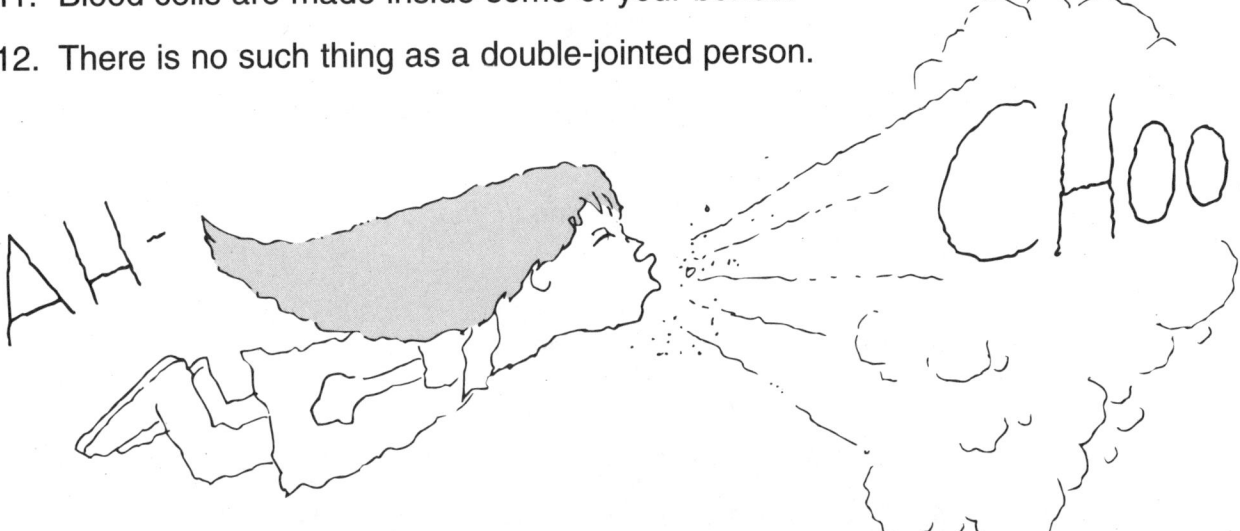

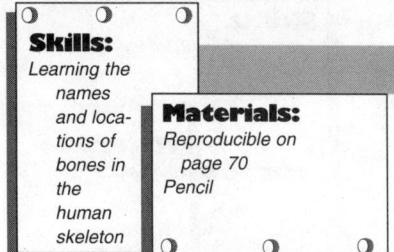

Skills: Learning the names and locations of bones in the human skeleton

Materials: Reproducible on page 70, Pencil

THE HUMAN BODY

Find the Bone

Write your name in the top right corner of your page. In this lesson we will learn the names of some of the bones in the human skeleton. You can see numbered blanks on your paper, with each one pointing to a different part of the skeleton. Listen carefully to my descriptions so that you can label the picture correctly.

(Teacher: You may wish to spell the italicized names for students.)

A. Let's begin with the breastbone. It is the center of the chest, and many of the ribs attach to it. Find the blank that points to this bone. Its proper name is *sternum*. Write this word in the correct blank.

B. Now skip to the thigh. This thighbone is called the femur, and it is the longest bone in your body. Find the correct blank, and write the word *femur* in it.

C. Next, look at the skeleton's forehead. This large plate is called the *frontal bone*. Label the blank for this bone at the top of your picture.

D. Now look at the forearms. Notice there is a large, main bone and a smaller one. The larger bone is called the *radius*. Find the proper blank and label this bone. The smaller bone is called the *ulna*. Label this bone as well.

E. Look at the skeleton's feet. You should find a blank that points to the ankle bones. These are called the *tarsals*. Label the ankle bones with this word.

F. Next, go back to the shoulder area. You should see the collarbone which goes from the neck out toward the shoulders. This is called the *clavicle*. Label this bone.

G. Now find the kneecap. The proper name for this bone is the *patella*. Write this word in the correct blank.

H. Move back up to the head. Notice the blanks that point to the jaws. The upper jaw is called the *maxilla*. The lower jaw is called the *mandible*. Label these two parts of the skeleton.

I. Now look at the lower leg. As in the lower arm, you should find two bones, a larger one and a smaller one. The larger bone, sometimes called the shinbone, is known as the *tibia*. Label the blank for this bone. The smaller bone is the *fibula*. Label this also.

J. The upper arm bone is another long bone in your body. It is called the *humerus*. Label this bone.

K. The tiny bones in your fingers and toes are called *phalanges*. Write the word *phalanges* in the blanks that point to both your fingers and toes.

You should now have filled all 15 blanks on your worksheet. Begin to use the new words you have learned when talking about the bones in your body!

(Teacher: For more practice in learning the names and locations of the bones, use the next lesson.)

THE HUMAN BODY

Bone Fractures

Skills:
Completing bone names
Giving bone locations

Materials:
Lined paper
Pencil

Number your paper from 1 to 10. For each line I will give you part of the spelling of the name of a bone from your skeleton page. Write the letters and blanks as I read them to you. Then try to complete the bone name by supplying the missing letters. Then, on the same line, tell in what part of the body this bone is found.

1. M _ _ IL _ _
2. _ LN _
3. T _ _ _ A
4. H U _ _ _ U S
5. _ _ MUR

6. _ _ TEL _ _
7. F _ _ U _ A
8. _ _ ERN _ _
9. C L _ _ IC _ _
10. _ _ D _ U S

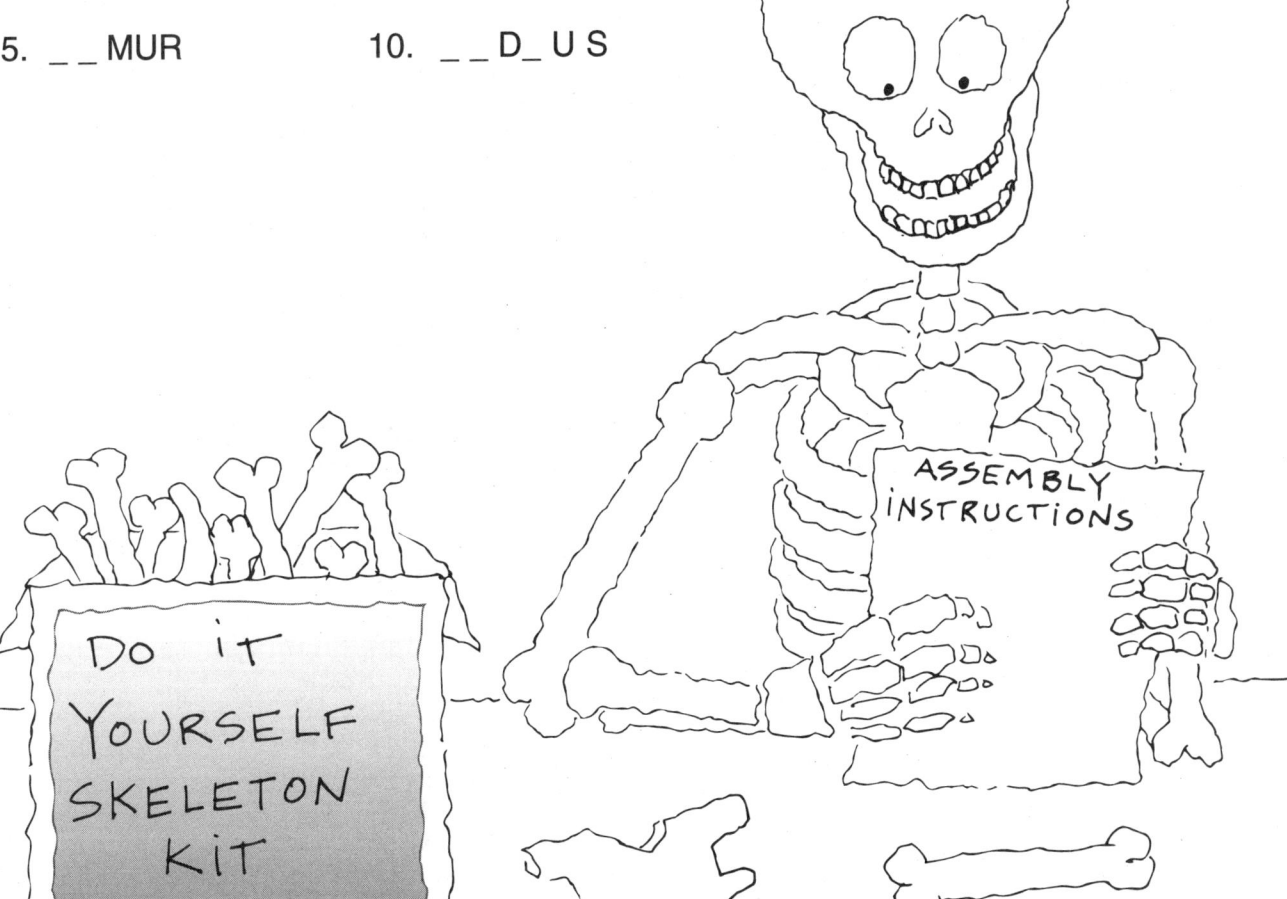

Find the Bone

Reproducible for use with page 68.

1. _____
2. _____
3. _____
4. _____
5. _____
6. _____
7. _____
8. _____
9. _____
10. _____
11. _____
12. _____
13. _____
14. _____
15. _____

THE HUMAN BODY

Skills: Recognizing parts of the body used by the senses

Materials: Lined paper, Pencil

Be "Sense"ible

The human body uses many specialized parts in order to see, smell, hear, taste and touch. How well do you know these parts? Make five columns across the top of your page by writing these words at the top: *sight, hearing, taste, smell, touch*. I will read several body parts. Your job is to write each one under the correct column. Some words may go in more than one place.

1. tongue
2. eardrum
3. pupil
4. nerves
5. skin
6. taste bud
7. hammer
8. brain
9. nostril
10. lens
11. stirrup
12. iris

Write your name at the bottom of your page.

Skills: Understanding how the heart works

Materials:
Reproducible on page 73
Pencil
Colored pencils: red, blue

THE HUMAN BODY

Heart Smart

You already know that your heart keeps your blood flowing. It is really a pump, working to push blood through the miles and miles of blood vessels that reach every part of your body. In this lesson we learn more about how the heart works.

Look at the drawing of the heart on your worksheet. Notice that the right and left sides are labeled as if you are facing the heart. Each upper side has two chambers, or sections. There is an upper chamber and a lower chamber on each side.

On each side, blood flows from the upper to the lower chamber. Little valves open and close to let the blood flow down. Each upper chamber is called an atrium. Label the *left atrium* and the *right atrium*. The lower chambers are called ventricles. Label the *left ventricle* and the *right ventricle*.

Blood is always filling both sides of the heart. The blood that fills the left side comes from your lungs. It travels into your heart through big blood vessels called *veins*. Veins are tubes that carry blood *into* the heart. This blood is bright red because it has just received a fresh supply of oxygen from the air you inhaled. Lightly shade both chambers of the left side of the heart with your red pencil to represent this bright red blood. The red blood goes from the upper to the lower chamber. Then it is pumped out of your heart through a big artery called the *aorta*. All *arteries* carry blood *away* from the heart. From big arteries, the blood travels through smaller and smaller arteries on its way through your body.

Blood that fills the right side of your heart has just finished making a trip through your body. It has turned a dark bluish color because it has given oxygen to the cells. The bluish blood enters your heart through great veins and flows from the right atrium to the ventricle. Lightly shade both chambers on the right side of the heart with your blue pencil to represent the "used" bluish blood. It is pumped out of your heart through an artery to your lungs.

In the lungs, the bluish blood collects oxygen from the air you inhale. It gives up the waste gas, carbon dioxide, which you exhale. The fresh oxygen makes the blood bright red again. The blood is now ready to be pumped out again by the heart for another trip through your body.

Heart Smart

Reproducible for use with page 72.

Your Heart and How It Works

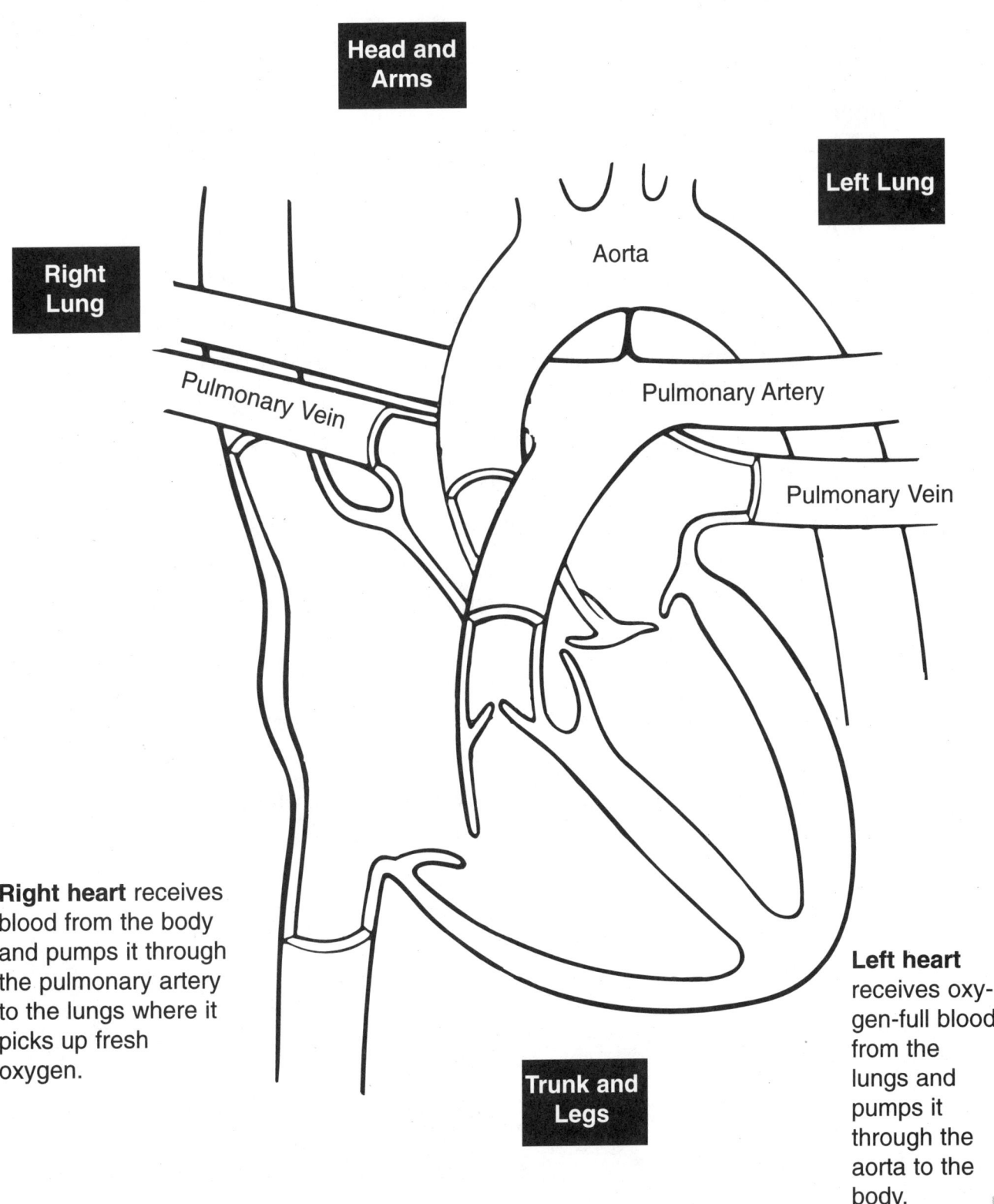

Right heart receives blood from the body and pumps it through the pulmonary artery to the lungs where it picks up fresh oxygen.

Left heart receives oxygen-full blood from the lungs and pumps it through the aorta to the body.

TLC10182 Copyright © Teaching & Learning Company, Carthage, IL 62321-0010

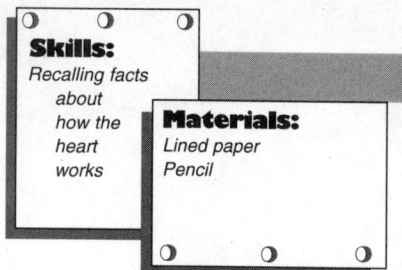

Skills: Recalling facts about how the heart works

Materials: Lined paper, Pencil

THE HUMAN BODY

Heart Choice

(Teacher: It may be helpful to have students complete the preceding lesson before attempting this one.)

Number your paper from 1 to 10. Let's see how much you remember about how the heart works. For each number I will read a question. I will also give you a choice of three possible answers. Write just the letter of the answer on your paper.

1. How many chambers are there all together in your heart?
   A. 2   B. 4   C. 5

2. What are the names of the upper and lower chambers?
   A. atrium and ventricle   B. aorta and vein   C. veins

3. What are the big vessels that carry blood into your heart called?
   A. pumps   B. arteries   C. veins

4. What is the name for vessels that carry blood away from your heart?
   A. arteries   B. veins   C. atriums

5. Blood turns bright red when it gets a fresh supply of what?
   A. carbon dioxide   B. oxygen   C. valves

6. What color does blood turn when it has traveled through your body and gathered waste products?
   A. green   B. pale pink   C. bluish red

7. In what direction does blood flow inside your heart?
   A. from top to bottom   B. from side to side   C. from bottom to top

8. In what part of your body does blood pick up its fresh supply of oxygen?
   A. brain   B. stomach   C. lungs

9. The waste in blood is exhaled as what gas?
   A. oxygen   B. carbon dioxide   C. helium

10. Write your name at number 10.

74

TLC10182 Copyright © Teaching & Learning Company, Carthage, IL 62321-0010

THE HUMAN BODY

A Beating Heart

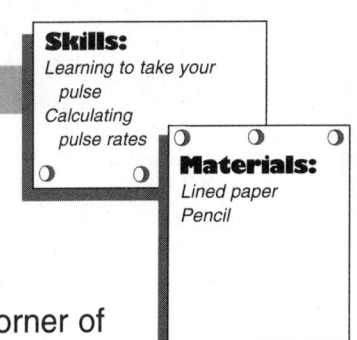

Skills:
Learning to take your pulse
Calculating pulse rates

Materials:
Lined paper
Pencil

Number your paper from 1 to 10. Write your name in the top right corner of your page. The beating of your heart is the sound it makes as it pumps the blood throughout your body. You can easily count your own heart beats. You can feel them in your wrist, which is called "taking your pulse." Place the first two fingers of your right hand on the inner side of your left wrist. Now you can feel a little jump every time your heart beats. The number of "jumps" you feel in a minute is the same as your heart rate.

Let's all try to take our own pulse for one minute. I will watch the time while you count the number of beats you feel.

Now we will spend three minutes running in place. Stand beside your seat and quietly jog in place. Now sit down and find your pulse. I will time you again for one minute. Write this heart rate on line 2. Was it faster that in line 1?

Often when a doctor or nurse takes your pulse, she checks it for a shorter length of time. If a nurse counts 50 beats in 30 seconds, how could she figure out your heart rate? Yes, she could multiply the number of heartbeats by 2, since there are two 30-second periods in one minute. Your heart rate would be 50 x 2, or 100 beats per minute. Nurses often check heart rates at 6, 10, 15 and 20 seconds also.

Now listen to these examples. Calculate the heartbeats per minute for each one.

3. Henry's heart beats 30 times in 20 seconds. What is his heart rate per minute?

4. Hattie's heart beats 20 times in 10 seconds. What is her heart rate per minute?

5. Hank's pulse is 45 beats in 30 seconds. What is his heart rate per minute?

6. Haley's pulse is 24 beats in 15 seconds. What is her heart rate per minute?

7. Herb's heart beats 8 times in 6 seconds. What is his heart rate per minute?

8. Holly's pulse is 35 beats in 20 seconds. What is her heart rate per minute?

9. Harry's heart beats 12 times in 10 seconds. What is his heart rate per minute?

10. Hilda's heart beats 19 times in 15 seconds. What is her heart rate per minute?

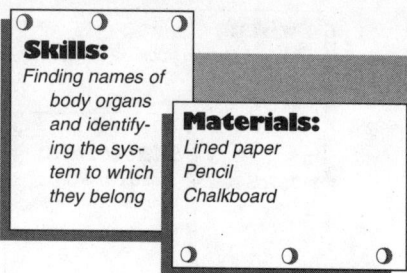

Skills: Finding names of body organs and identifying the system to which they belong

Materials: Lined paper, Pencil, Chalkboard

THE HUMAN BODY

"Organ"ization!

Write your name in the top right corner of your page. Number your paper from 1 to 10, skipping a line between each number. For each number, I will read you a set of letters. Write each letter in exactly the order that I read it. Then look at the letters you've written and figure out what two body parts are hidden there. To find the body organs, simply separate the two words, without changing the order of any letters. Write the two words under your set of letters.

Both hidden body parts work together in the same system to help perform the same job. You will find these systems in this lesson.

(Teacher: Write these on the board for students' reference.)

Nervous system–N   Respiratory system–R
Circulatory system–C   Skeletal system–S
Digestive system–D   Muscular system–M

Write the first letter of each system next to your separated words in each line. For example, if you wrote the letters B E R Y A I E N, you could separate them and spell the words *brain* and *eye*. (Show this on the chalkboard.) These organs work together to help you see, and they are part of the nervous system. So you would write *N* beside the two words. Now it's your turn.

1. L U N O N G S E S
2. F U E L M U N A R
3. A V E O R I T A N
4. T E B I N C D E P O N S
5. I M N T O E S U T T I N H E
6. S B P I R A N A L C I N O R D
7. A R H E T E A R R Y T
8. R H U A M E D I R U U S S
9. S L I T O V E M A R C H
10. L I T G A R I M E C E N P T S

THE HUMAN BODY

Oddly Enough

Skills: Classification

Materials: Lined paper, Pencil

Number your paper from 1 to 15. For each line, I will read a set of four words. There will be one word in each set that does not belong with the others. Write this odd word on your numbered line. The set of words that belong together may be organs of the body in the same system, bones that are connected to one another or may have features related to the human body.

1. stomach, ear, esophagus, pancreas
2. hair, nose, eye, tongue
3. skull, spine, pelvis, biceps
4. epidermis, blood, pore, follicle
5. enamel, root, crown, jaw
6. hammer, pupil, iris, retina
7. lung, aorta, vein, artery
8. mandible, ulna, frontal bone, maxilla
9. eardrum, anvil, lens, stirrup
10. tendon, ligament, cartilage, brain
11. trachea, lung, liver, diaphragm
12. clavicle, femur, tibia, fibula
13. red blood cells, platelets, white blood cells, arteries
14. elbow, rib, knee, shoulder
15. ulna, humerus, patella, radius

Write your name at the bottom of the page.

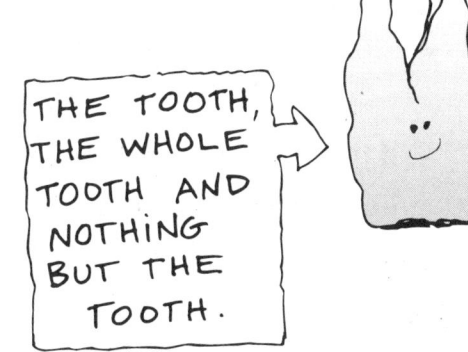

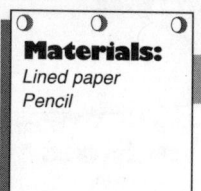

Materials:
Lined paper
Pencil

PRE/POSTTEST FOR PART 6

The Solar System

Write your name in the top right corner of your page. Number your paper from 1 to 10. Follow the directions for each line.

1. Write the names of the nine planets in our solar system in order from the one closest to the one farthest from the sun.

2. The sun has a surface temperature of about 6000°C and is a yellow star. What color is the hottest stars that are 21,000°C?

3. One astronomical unit is equal to the distance from the _____ to the _____. Write the missing words on line 3 of your page.

4. If the distance from the sun to the Earth is 1.0, the distance from the sun to Mars is about what?

For numbers 5-7, write S if I'm describing the sun. Write E if I'm describing the Earth, and write M if I'm describing the moon. You may write more than one letter for each statement.

5. It resolves around the Earth.

6. It rotates on its axis.

7. It has an atmosphere.

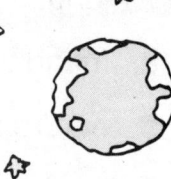

For number 8, write these numbers on the line: 8, 25, 60 and 400. Circle the number that tells how many minutes it takes for light produced by the sun to reach the Earth. Underline the number of days it takes for the sun to make one rotation on its axis.

9. What is another name for a "shooting star"?

10. Make three columns on the next five lines of your paper. Write these five words in the first column: *black, Milky, asteroid, solar, Halley's*. Write these five words in the second column: *Way, Comet, hole, giant, eclipse*. Now draw lines to match a word from the first column with a word in the second column to spell the name of an object or event in space. There will be one extra in each column. Write the final compound words or phrases in the third column.

11. Look at the words you made in number 10. Find the name for an event that occurs when the moon is directly between the Earth and the sun, and the sun seems to disappear. Underline this name. Find the name of our galaxy. Circle it.

THE SOLAR SYSTEM

Planetary Order

Skills: Learning the order of the planets

Materials: Chalkboard, Paper, Pencil

Use as a warm-up for Part 6.

(Teacher: Write the names of the planets on the chalkboard in order: Mercury, Venus, Earth, Mars, Jupiter, Saturn, Uranus, Neptune, Pluto.)

You will see the names of the nine planets in our solar system on the board. They are written in order, from the one closest to the sun to the one farthest from the sun. In this lesson, you should try to memorize that planets in this order.

1. For the first activity you will compose a sentence to help you remember the order of the planets. Notice that the first letters of the planets are: M, V, E, M, J, S, U, N and P. Use these same initials to begin words that form a sentence or a phrase that you can remember. Here are some examples:
   Many very energetic, jumping singers used new pianos.
   My very elderly mother just sewed unusually neat patches.

On your paper write two or three sentences of your own. Choose your favorite to share with the class.

(Teacher: Call on each student to read their sentence aloud. Ask the rest of the class to listen carefully to make sure each sentence is correct. For extra fun and challenge, secretly ask a few students to purposely make mistakes in their sentences. For instance, Johnny could read this sentence: "Mary visits every Monday, juggling some new plates." Check to see if students are listening closely enough to realize that Johnny omitted the letter U for Uranus.)

2. For the next activity, I will erase the planet names from the board. I will read a list of planets, leaving out one or two of them. Raise your hand as soon as you know which planet or planets I have left out. *Do this several times, omitting different planets.*

3. For the final practice, I will call four of you to the chalkboard at a time. I will read the letters of planet in a scrambled order. Write down the letters just as I read them. Underneath that set of letters, quickly write the name of the planet correctly, beginning with a capital letter. Beside that write the number (1-9) that tells in which place it is from the sun. *(For example: H E R A T = EARTH, 3)* Try to be the first one to write the name correctly with the right number. When you are not at the chalkboard, watch the others carefully and help decide if they have the correct answer.

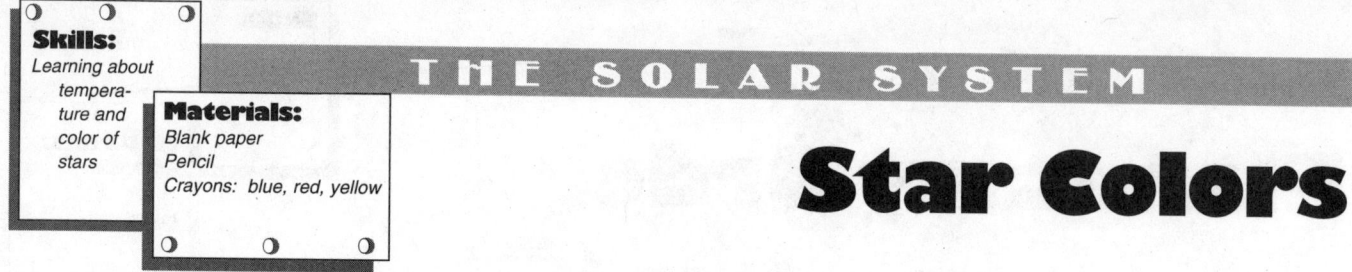

Skills: Learning about temperature and color of stars

Materials: Blank paper, Pencil, Crayons: blue, red, yellow

THE SOLAR SYSTEM

Star Colors

In this lesson you will learn how the temperature of a star affects its color. Draw four large circles on your page, two at the top and two at the bottom. These will represent four stars.

Our star is a yellow star. Its surface temperature is about 6000°C or 10,000°F. In the top right circle, write the word *Sun*. Label its temperature as 6000°C. Color it yellow.

Some stars are cooler than the sun. One example is a star called Antares. Its temperature is half the temperature of the sun. In the top left circle, write the word *Antares*. Write in its temperature. This star, as well as others at the same temperature, appears red in the sky, so color this circle red.

Many stars are hotter than our sun. Stars that are 1000°C hotter than the sun appear as white stars. Label the lower left-hand circle with the correct temperature. Leave it white.

There are stars in the universe that are three times hotter than white starts. They appear to be blue. Color your last circle blue, and label it with the correct temperature. Write your name under the blue circle.

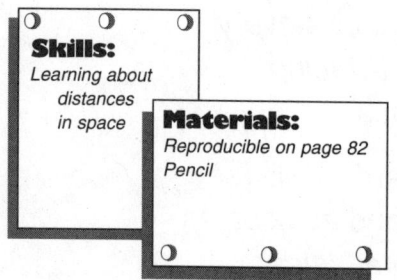

Skills: Learning about distances in space

Materials: Reproducible on page 82, Pencil

Long Distance

(Teacher: Before beginning this lesson, make sure students know how to read and write numbers in millions and billions.)

Write your name in the top left corner of your page. In this lesson, you will complete a chart that shows distances in space, from the sun to each of the planets in our solar system. The planets are listed in the first column, in order from those the closest to those farthest from the sun.

First fill in the names of the missing planets, placing them in the right order and spelling them correctly.

THE SOLAR SYSTEM

Long Distance

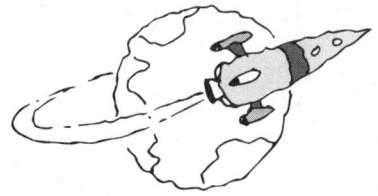

Next, I will explain the other three columns in the chart.

- Column A shows the distance from the sun to each planet in miles. You can see that Earth is approximately 93 million miles away.

- Column B shows the same distance, written in kilometers rather than miles. Remember that one mile is about 1.6 kilometers, so the numbers in column B will be larger than the numbers in column A. The Earth is about 149,600,000 kilometers from the sun.

- Column C shows another way to measure the same distance. Here we are using a length which is called an astronomical unit. This is equal to the distance from Earth to the sun. So in column C for Earth, you should write 1.0. You can see that with the large distances in space, that the astronomical unit is easier to use than the distances measured in either miles or kilometers.

Now I will read you the remainder of the missing numbers for your chart. Listen carefully as you fill in the blank spaces on your page.

We'll begin with figures for column A: Venus–67,240,000 miles; Jupiter–483,880,000 miles; Saturn–887,140,000 miles; Uranus–1,783,980,000 miles; Pluto–3,666,000,000 miles.

Next, we will complete column B: Mercury–57,900,000; Mars–227,900,000; Saturn–1,427,000,000; Neptune–4,497,000,000.

Based on the numbers in columns A and B, try to estimate the numbers for column C. Write your predictions lightly in pencil in column C. *(Teacher: Allow a few minutes for discussion and for students to make their predictions.)*

Now listen to the correct number of astronomical units and write them clearly in your chart. Mercury–0.4; Venus–0.7; Mars–1.5; Jupiter–5.2; Saturn–9.5; Uranus–19.2; Neptune–30.0; Pluto–39.4.

Finally, read the sentence at the bottom of the page. Fill in the blanks. Double-check your work as you listen to me read the completed sentence: *One astronomical unit is equal to the distance from the Earth to the sun.*

TLC10182 Copyright © Teaching & Learning Company, Carthage, IL 62321-0010

Long Distance

Reproducible for use with pages 80 and 81.

\	Average Distance from the Sun		
Planet	A. Miles	B. Kilometers	C. Astronomical Units
Mercury	36,000,000		
		108,200,000	
Earth	93,000,000	149,600,000	
	141,710,000		
Jupiter		778,300,000	
Saturn			
		2,870,000,000	
Neptune	2,796,460,000		
		5,900,000,000	

One astronomical unit is equal to the _____ from the _____ to the _____.

THE SOLAR SYSTEM

Chart Check

Skills: Reading and interpreting a chart

Materials: Completed chart from previous lesson, Pencil, Paper

Number your paper from 1 to 10. Write your answer to each question on the correct line. Use the right-hand side of your paper for work space as needed.

1. Which planet is 30 times further away from the sun than the Earth?
2. Which planet is about 100,000,000 kilometers away from the sun?
3. Which planet is nearly 900,000,000 miles away from the sun?
4. Which planet is just over five times further from the sun than the Earth?
5. Which two consecutive planets have the biggest space between them?
6. About how many miles separate Mercury and Pluto?
7. How many kilometers separate Earth and Mars?
8. Which planet is closer to Earth, Venus or Mars?
9. Which planet is closer to Jupiter, Mars or Saturn?
10. Write your name at number 10.

WHEW! THAT'S A LONG, LONG WAY!

THE SOLAR SYSTEM

Which Body?

Skills: Distinguishing features of the sun, Earth and moon

Materials: Lined paper, Pencil

Write your name in the top left corner of your page. Number from 1 to 15. For each number, I will read a statement. You need to decide if it describes the sun, Earth or moon. If it describes the sun, write S on the line. If it describes the Earth, write E on the line. If it tells about the moon, write M on the line. Note: Some statements may fit more than one of these bodies. In that case, write every letter that is correct.

1. It is about 93 million miles away from Earth.
2. It revolves around the Earth.
3. It rotates on its axis.
4. It is the controlling body of our solar system.
5. About three-fourths of its surface is covered with water.
6. It revolves around the sun.
7. Its surface contains craters.
8. This body is the main cause of tides on the Earth.
9. Day and night on Earth are determined by this body.
10. Part of its surface contains mountains that are rocky.
11. Its orbit is elliptical in shape.
12. Its diameter is just over 2000 miles.
13. It has an atmosphere.
14. All the elements in this body are gases.
15. Soil forms on its surface.

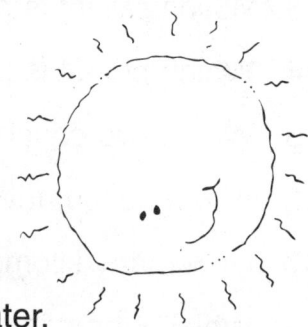

I'M SO BRIGHT, MY MOM CALLS ME SON!

THE SOLAR SYSTEM

Sunny Numbers

Skills: Learning numerical facts about the sun

Materials: Reproducible on page 87, Pencil

Write your name in the top right corner of your worksheet. In this lesson we will study a lot of interesting facts and numbers about the sun. First I will read you nine numbers which you need to copy in the lettered blanks at the top of your page.

A. 8	D. 175	G. 865,000
B. 25	E. 400	H. 35,000,000
C. 60	F. 10,000	I. 93,000,000

Now read the statements listed on your paper. Find the correct number from your list of nine choices and write it in the blank. Also add the correct label. We will go through these statements one at a time.

1. Find the diameter of the sun in miles and label it with the word *miles*.

2. What is the distance from the Earth to the sun in miles? Find the number and label it.

3. Can you guess about how many minutes it takes for light produced by the sun to reach us here on Earth? Choose the number that tells how many minutes and label it. Hint: It is 499 seconds.

4. Do you remember from an earlier lesson what the temperature is on the the surface of the sun? Find the number that tells how many degrees Fahrenheit the temperature is and label it.

5. Next, predict which number tells the internal temperature of the sun. This number is also in degrees Fahrenheit. Fill in the number and label it.

6. There have been a number of elements identified in the gases burning in the sun. Can you guess how many? It is close to one of the numbers above. Write the number in your blank.

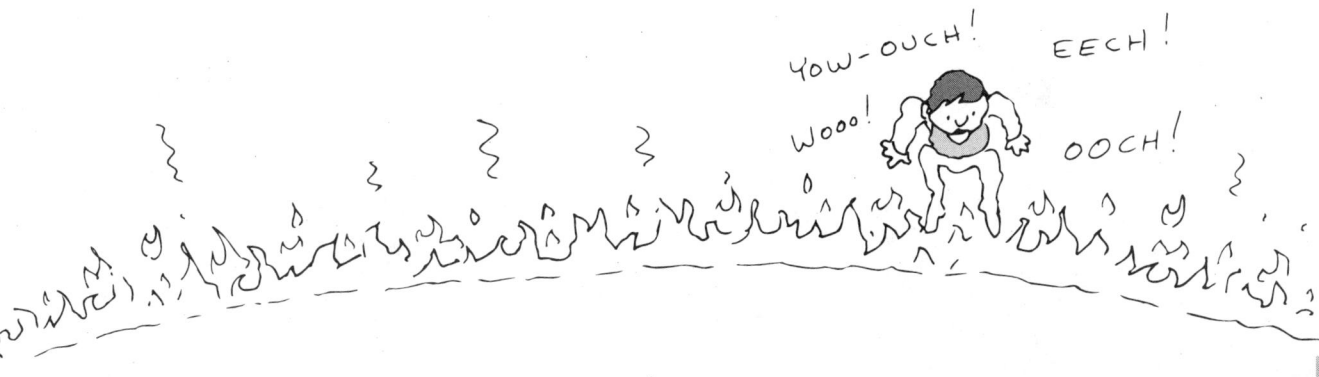

TLC10182 Copyright © Teaching & Learning Company, Carthage, IL 62321-0010

85

THE SOLAR SYSTEM

Sunny Numbers

7. You already know that the Earth is constantly moving, but do you know that the sun is moving, too? We are part of the Milky Way galaxy which is a spiraling group of stars and planets. Our sun is constantly in motion. It moves at a certain number of miles per second. Find that number and label it *miles per second.*

8. The sun also rotates on its axis. It takes a set of number of days to make one rotation. Try to figure out how many. Label your number with the word *days.*

9. The sun's diameter is many times larger than the Earth's or moon's. Can you guess how many times larger? If many moons were placed edge to edge across the diameter of the sun, how many moons would it take to reach the entire distance? Find the number.

10. By now you should have used all nine numbers at the top of your page, but you should have one more statement remaining. You need to do your own calculations for this in the space at the bottom of your page. As the statement says, you need to find how long it would take to drive your car from the Earth to the sun, supposing this were actually possible, if you drove an average speed of 55 miles per hour for 24 hours a day. You will want to use your calculator for this, and you will need to round off numbers as you work. Here is one way you can find out.

   - First, recall the total distance. *(It is about 93,000,000 miles.)*

   - Secondly, figure out how many miles you could drive in one 24-hour day. *(24 x 55 = 1320 miles)*

   - Next, divide the total distance by the number of miles per day to learn how many days you would need to drive. *(93,000,000 ÷ 1320 = 70,455 days)*

   - Finally, divide that number of days by 365 to see how many years are in that number of days. *(70,455 ÷ 365 = 193 years)* Write your final answer in the blank.

Sunny Numbers

Reproducible for use with pages 85 and 86.

A. _____   D. _____   G. _____
B. _____   E. _____   H. _____
C. _____   F. _____   I. _____

1. Diameter of the sun _____

2. Distance from the Earth to the sun _____

3. The light from the sun takes _____ to reach us.

4. Temperature on the surface of the sun _____

5. Internal temperature of the sun _____

6. The approximate number of elements found in the sun _____

7. As part of the rotating Milky Way system, the sun moves at the rate of
_____.

8. The sun rotates on its axis once every _____.

9. It would take _____ moons edge to edge to reach across the sun.

10. If you were to drive a car at 55 m.p.h. from the Earth to the sun, it would take
_____.

TLC10182 Copyright © Teaching & Learning Company, Carthage, IL 62321-0010

Skills: Following directions

Materials:
Lined paper
Pencil

THE SOLAR SYSTEM

Star Shift

Have you ever seen a "shooting star"? You may have seen a bright streak of light moving through the sky. This is caused when a very small body of matter enters the Earth's atmosphere. Find out the scientific name for a shooting star by following these directions.

Write your name in the top right corner of your page. Number from 1 to 12. For each line I will read you an instruction. Write the letters that remain after you follow each step.

1. Print the words SHOOTING STAR clearly on your paper. Leave out the space between the two words.
2. Delete every S.
3. Delete each O.
4. Insert an E after the second consonant.
5. Delete the last vowel.
6. Insert an O between the fifth and sixth consonants.
7. Delete the third consonant from the right.
8. Replace the first T with an M.
9. Remove the second vowel from the left.
10. Insert an E after the fourth consonant from the left.
11. Remove the fifth letter from the right.
12. Remove the first letter.

Now you know! Another name for a shooting star is a *meteor*. When it lands on Earth, it is called a *meteorite*.

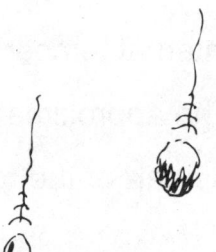
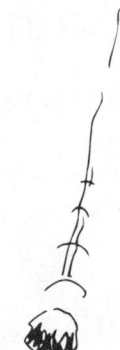

THE SOLAR SYSTEM

Astronomical Matchup

Skills: Astronomy terminology

Materials: Lined paper, Pencil

Outer space is full of unusual objects, occurrences and weather. In this lesson you will need to piece 11 of them together. First write your name in the top left corner.

First divide your paper into three columns. Number from 1 to 11. Write these words in the first column: *black, sun, asteroid, meteor, solar, northern, Halley's, Big, Milky, dwarf* and *super.*

Write these words in the second column: *Way, lights, eclipse, spots, hole, Dipper, giant, belt, shower, star* and *Comet.*

Next draw lines to match a word in the first column with a word in the second to spell the name of something in space. You will form either compound words or two-word phrases.

Finally, write the completed words or phrases in alphabetical order in the third column, again skipping a line between words.

(Teacher: End the lesson here, or continue on to this additional activity.)

Now look over the words you have written in the third column, and follow these instructions.

- A. Find the name of a constellation. Circle it.
- B. Find the name for an event that occurs when the moon is directly between the Earth and the sun, and the sun seems to disappear. Underline this name.
- C. Find the name for a region from which matter and energy cannot escape that results from the collapse of a massive star group. Draw a box around this name.
- D. Find the name for a very large star. Draw a circle after this name.
- E. Find the name of our galaxy. Draw a wavy line underneath it.
- F. Find the name for a group of tiny orbiting bodies located between Mars and Jupiter. Draw a wavy line above it.
- G. Find the name for a very small star that may be no larger than Earth. Put a star beside this name.

(Encourage students to do some research and learn more about these objects and events.)

Answer Key

Pre/Posttest, Part 1, page 10

Name in top right corner.
1. Person
2. Person
3. Computer
4. Top
5. Left
6. home row
7. dog–7
8. butter–10
9. Answers will vary. Possible outcomes: LONG, THIS ARGUE, etc.
10.

	A	B	C	D	E
1	13	10	15		
2	25	14	11	50	
3	17	17	13		
4	26	21	24		
5					
6			63		

11.-13. Answers will vary. Here are some possible outcomes.
   alphabetically by name–Bond
   chronologically by birth date–Stone
   alphabetically by state–White
   chronologically by zip–Stone
14. mouse
15. data base
16. program

More Keyboarding, page 14

Answers will vary. Here are some possible outcomes.
1. first name
2. last name
3. cot
4. pen
5. bat
6. oil
7. hall, flask
8. boot
9. more
10. proper, true
11. pony, lollipop
12. grass, vest

In and Out, page 17

Table 1
1. 1   23
2. 11   35
3. 25   77
4. 4   14
5. 10   32

Table 2
6. broom   7
7. yellow   8
8. nothing   9
9. in   3
10. too   5

(Many other answers are possible here.)

Table 3
11. VQ   UP
12. SBU   RAT
13. MJLF   LIKE
14. PME   OLD
15. GSPH   FROG

Table 4
16. 12   4
17. 20   6
18. 40   11
19. 28   8
20. 36   10

Table 5
Rule: Subtract 1, divide by 3.
21. 16   5
22. 25   8
23. 100   33
24. 13   4
25. 40   13

Table 6
Rule: Use the first two letters in the day of the week that follows the day given.
26. MO   TU
27. FR   SA
28. WE   TH
29. SU   MO
30. TH   FR

Variations may be possible in stating the rules for Tables 5 and 6.

Spread It! page 19

	A	B	C	D	E	F	G
1	Name					Date	
2							
3				Title			
4							
5	class	Monday	Tuesday	Wednesday	Thursday	Friday	
6	Smith	22	24	22	20	21	109
7	Jones	23	25	20	21	22	
8	Green	20	15	18	20	16	
9	Brown	18	20	15	13	14	80
10		83	84				

Data Details, pages 20-21

11. Ball, Yates
12. Stone, Miller, 5
13. 4, Fisher, Rich
14. 4, Ball, white
15. 3, Long, Brown
16. White, Bond
17. Answers will vary. It could sort secondly by putting cities or last names in alphabetical order.

Computer Scramble, page 22

1. Name
2. mouse
3. input
4. hardware
5. modem
6. disc
7. printer
8. virus
9. binary
10. data base
11. software
12. program
13. memory
14. flowchart
15. megabyte

Pre/Posttest, Part 2, page 23

Name in top right corner.

1. Answers will vary.
2. D, B, A, C
3. K
4. P
5. true
6. true
7. false
8. calories
9. lose
10. fat
11. renewable
12. destroyed
13.-14. Answers will vary.

Sarah's Source, page 24

Students should have found these 14 items in the story: clock radio, water heater, hair dryer, curling iron, refrigerator, toaster, microwave, dishwasher, clothes dryer, clothes washer, television, light, CD player, doorbell.

Current News, page 26

Name in top left corner.

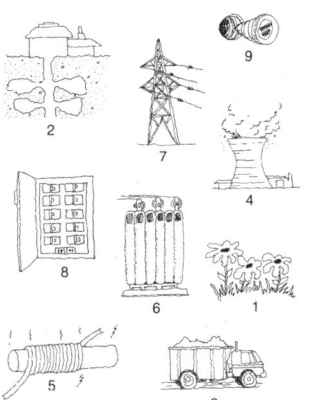

Get to Work! page 27

Answers will vary. Here are some possible outcomes.

1. rotating blades on a fan
2. Ferris wheel in motion
3. swinging swing
4. clothes dryer tumbling
5. swinging pendulum on a clock
6. clothes washer that's turned off
7. child ready to go down a slide
8. computer printer ready to do a job
9. idle roller skate
10. basketball setting on a shelf
11. skier going down a ski slope
12. wind-up toy being started
13. fly ball being caught by a baseball player
14. spinning top being stopped
15. Name

Four Forms, pages 28-29

Name in top right corner.

1. R
2. M
3. C
4. T
5. C
6. M
7. R
8. C
9. true
10. true
11. false
12. true
13. false
14. true
15. true

Counting Calories, page 32

Name in top right corner.
Student's completed reproducible should look like this. Menus for the lunches, of course, will vary.

Dairy Products	
Food and Amount	Calories
whole milk, 1 cup	150
skim milk, 1 cup	85
chocolate milk shake, 1 cup	300
cottage cheese, 1 cup	215

Meat, Poultry and Fish	
lean roast beef, 3 oz.	160
pork chop, 3 oz.	270
roast chicken, 3 oz. white	140
fish sticks, each one	70

Grains	
plain bagel, one	200
whole wheat bread, one slice	65
bran muffin, one	140
oatmeal, 1 cup	145
corn cereal, 1 oz.	110
pretzel sticks, 10	10
doughnut, one	220
chocolate chip cookies, 4	180

Fruits and Vegetables	
Food and Amount	Calories
apple, one fresh	80
banana, one	105
orange juice, 1 cup	110
raisins, 1 cup	440
strawberries, 1 cup plain	45
green beans, 1 cup cooked	35
carrot, one raw	30
celery, one stalk	5
sweet corn, one ear	85
baked potato, one peeled	145
mashed potatoes, 1 cup	160
potato salad, 1 cup	360
tomato soup, 1 cup	160

Miscellaneous	
margarine, 1 T.	100
sugar, 1 T.	45
jam, 1 T.	55

Stan's Breakfast	**Dan's Breakfast**
150 + 145 + 220 + 200 + 100 + 55 = (870 calories)	110 + 85 + 110 + 65 + 55 = (425 calories)

Stan's Lunch	**Dan's Lunch**
Sample: whole milk, pork chop, potato salad, sweet corn with margarine, banana, doughnut = 1290 calories	Sample: skim milk, roast beef, baked potato, green beans, carrot, strawberries, slice of bread with margarine, two chocolate chip cookies = 755 calories

Burning Up! page 33

Name in upper right corner.
1. sleeping–60
2. reading–100
3. driving–120
4. housework–180
5. slow cycling–210
6. swimming–300
7. roller skating–350
8. tennis–420
9. basketball–500
10. running–900

In and Out, page 34

1. 2400 calories
2. 3000 calories total; he would gain weight
3. 3170 calories
4. 2850 calories total; he would lose weight
5. Answer will vary. Here are two possibilities.
    A. skim milk, chicken sandwich (3 oz. chicken, 2 slices bread, margarine), tomato soup, apple, 2 cookies for a total of 785 calories
    B. skim milk, 4 fish sticks, baked potato with margarine, celery, strawberries for a total of 660 calories
6. Again, answers will vary. Possible outcomes include:
    A. swimming–1 hour, cycling–1 hour, housework–1 hour, sitting to read–1 hour (790 calories)
    B. tennis–1 hour, basketball–1/2 hour, driving–1 hour (790 calories)
7. Answers will vary.
8. Name and date

Renewability, page 35

1. R
2. N
3. R (Quick-growing forests are planted now.)
4. R
5. N
6. N
7. R
8. N
9. R
10. R
11. N
12. R
13. Name

Cross Out, page 37

Name in top right corner.
Answer: The law of conservation of energy says that energy cannot be created or destroyed. (It can only change forms and be transferred.)

Save It! page 38

Name in top right corner.
1. smile
2. smile
3. frown
4. frown
5. smile
6. smile
7. frown
8. smile
9. frown
10. frown
11. smile
12. frown
13. smile
14. smile
15. Answers will vary.

Pre/Posttest, Part 3, page 39

Name in top right corner.
1. Answers could include showering, laundry, drinking, cooking, etc.
2. Answers could include watering the lawn, growing food, producing electricity, etc.
3. 960 gallons
4. precipitation
5. evaporation
6. infiltration
7. Landlocked states are: Idaho, Nevada, Utah, Wyoming, Colorado, Arizona, New Mexico, Montana, North Dakota, South Dakota, Nebraska, Kansas, Oklahoma, Iowa, Mississippi, Arkansas, Kentucky, Tennessee, West Virginia and Vermont. (See **River Route** lesson on page 45.)
8. Any states not listed above.
9. cyclone
10. glacier
11. element
12. compound
13. hydrogen and oxygen

Water "Guess"timates, pages 41-42

Here is what a sample page may look like:

Shower	15 showers 10 minutes each = (150 minutes)	8 gallons	1200 gallons of water used in the shower per week
Toilet	15 flushes x 7 days = (105 flushes) per week	6 gallons	630 gallons of water used in the toilet per week
Washing Machine	10 loads	20 gallons	200 gallons of water used in the washer per week
Potatoes	10 pounds	23 gallons	230 gallons of water used to grow one week's worth of potatoes
Bread	2 loaves	150 gallons	300 gallons of water used for one week's worth of bread

Name at bottom.

The Water Cycle, page 43

Name in top right corner.

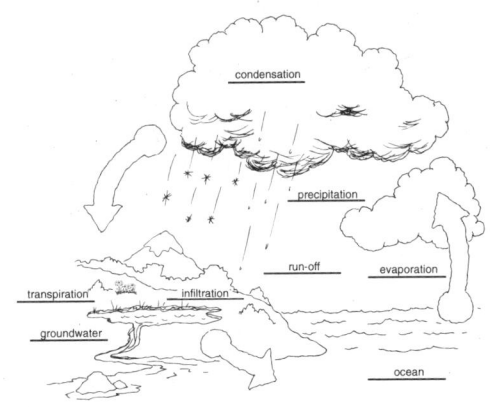

River Route, page 46

Name in top right corner.
Mileage of trip should be written under their name.
Considering only the major bodies of water shown on the map, there are 20 landlocked states. The are Idaho, Nevada, Utah, Wyoming, Colorado, Arizona, New Mexico, Montana, North Dakota, South Dakota, Nebraska, Kansas, Oklahoma, Iowa, Mississippi, Arkansas, Kentucky, Tennessee, West Virginia and Vermont.

Precipitation Puzzler, page 48

Name in top right.
1. temperature
2. blizzard
3. glacier
4. cyclone
5. hail
6. typhoon
7. drizzle
8. sleet
9. rain
10. thunder
11. tidal waves
12. flood
13. snow

Compound Matchup, page 51

1. E
2. G
3. D
4. A
5. I
6. H
7. H
8. F
9. C
10. B

Name at bottom.

Pre/Posttest, Part 4, page 53

Name in top right corner.
Date under name.
1. Vertebrates: cat, trout, toad
   Invertebrates: crab, bee
2. B, M
3. F, A, R, B, M
4. A
5. car, owl; cow
6. lamp, ball; lamb
7. The tapeworm at 33 feet is the longest.
8. opossum–mammal
9. bullfrog–amphibian
10. F
11. O
12. true
13. true

No Bones About It! page 54

V = Vertebrate, I = Invertebrate

1. V	6. V	11. V	16. V
2. I	7. V	12. I	17. I
3. V	8. I	13. I	18. V
4. I	9. I	14. V	19. V
5. I	10. V	15. I	20. I

Five Fits, page 54

2. M
3. F
4. B, M
5. F, A, R, B, M
6. A
7. B
8. M
9. M
10. F, A, R, B
11. B, M
12. M

Name at bottom.

A Long Time, page 57

Name in top left corner.

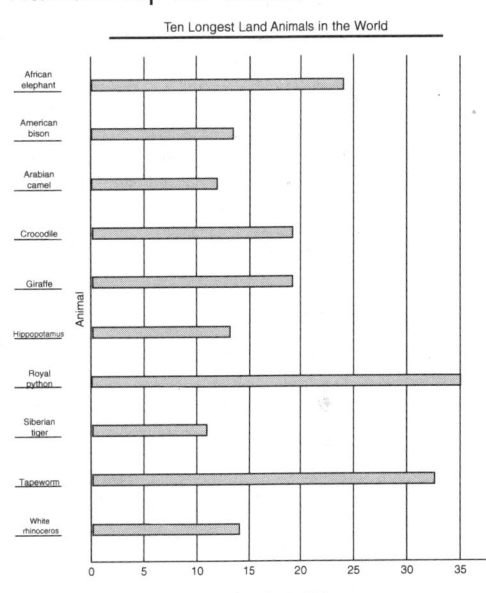

Fractured Mammals, page 58

Name in top right corner.
1. <u>ap</u>ple, <u>e</u>ar; ape
2. <u>b</u>lue, <u>at</u>tic; bat
3. <u>shee</u>t, <u>p</u>ig; sheep
4. <u>wh</u>ite, <u>al</u>l, <u>e</u>gg; whale
5. <u>sk</u>i, <u>un</u>cle, <u>k</u>ing; skunk
6. <u>go</u>at, <u>at</u>e; goat
7. <u>bea</u>ch, <u>ar</u>k; bear
8. <u>hor</u>izon, <u>see</u>saw; horse
9. <u>pup</u>il, <u>py</u>ramid; puppy
10. <u>mo</u>ney, <u>ke</u>ep, <u>y</u>es; monkey

Places, Please! page 60

Name in top left.
Write date under name.
1. hog, mammal
2. robin, bird
3. bobcat, mammal
4. butterfly, insect
5. falcon, bird
6. opossum, mammal
7. tortoise, reptile
8. salamander, amphibian
9. cricket, insect
10. beaver, mammal
11. firefly, insect
12. iguana, reptile
13. bullfrog, amphibian
14. sparrow, bird
15. earwig, insect

Find the Facts, page 62

Name in top right.
1. F
2. O
3. O
4. F
5. F
6. F
7. O
8. F
9. F
10. O
11. F
12. O
13. O
14. O
15. F

Logic Lines, page 64

Name in top right.
1. true
2. true
3. false
4. false
5. true
6. false
7. false
8. true
9. false
10. true
11. true
12. true

Pre/Posttest, Part 5, page 66

Name in top right.
1. true
2. false
3. A. femur, B. patella, C. tibia, F. phalanges
4. 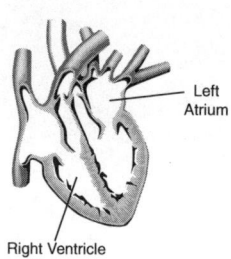 Left Atrium; Right Ventricle
5. femur
6. mandible
7. Circle: nerves, taste buds, brain, tongue
8. C
9. C
10. 96 beats per minute
11. stomach, liver; digestive system
12. aorta, vein; circulatory system
13. brain; the others all connect with bones in the skeletal system
14. liver; the others are part of the respiratory system.

Trivial True and False, page 67

1. False. The hardest substance is the enamel on teeth.
2. True. Babies have about 450 bones at birth. Many of these fuse together as they grow. Adults have only about 206 different bones.
3. False. It is made of 29 different bones.
4. True
5. False. Taste buds on the tongue tell you whether food is sweet, salty, etc. But without the smell received by your nose, food would have no flavor.
6. True. Gravity and daytime activity make us lose about 1/4" (.6 cm) during the day. While we sleep the cartilage between bones absorbs water from the rest of the body and puffs up again.
7. True
8. False. It weighs about three pounds.
9. False. You have 12 pairs of ribs in all. Only the first seven are attached to the breastbone. The next three pairs attach to cartilage at the ends of the other ribs. The last two pairs are held in place only by muscle tissue. These are called "floating" ribs.
10. True. Sometimes the air can travel up to 100 mph!

11. True. The substance inside bones which manufactures blood cells is called *marrow*.
12. True. People that can bend their thumb back or do the splits have very flexible ligaments that give them a wider range of movement than normal. There is no such thing as having two joints at the same place.

Bone Fractures, page 69

1. maxilla, upper jaw
2. ulna, forearm
3. tibia, lower leg
4. humerus, upper arm
5. femur, thigh
6. patella, kneecap
7. fibula, lower leg
8. sternum, chest
9. clavicle, collarbone
10. radius, forearm

Find the Bone, page 70

Name in top right.
1. frontal bone
2. maxilla
3. mandible
4. clavicle
5. sternum
6. humerus
7. ulna
8. radius
9. phalanges
10. femur
11. patella
12. tibia
13. fibula
14. tarsals
15. phalanges

Be "Sense"ible, page 71

sight	hearing	taste	smell	touch
pupil	eardrum	tongue	nerves	nerves
nerves	nerves	nerves	brain	skin
brain	hammer	taste bud	nostril	brain
lens	brain	brain		
iris	stirrup	nostril		

Name at bottom.

Heart Smart, page 73

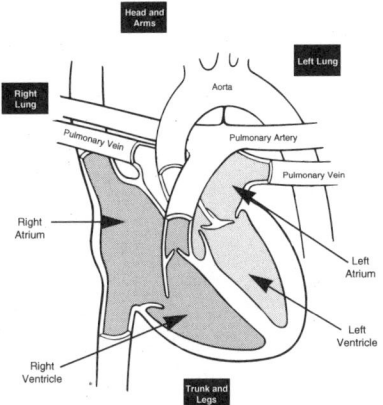

Heart Choice, page 74

1. B
2. A
3. C
4. A
5. B
6. C
7. A
8. C
9. B
10. Name

A Beating Heart, page 75

Name in top right.
1.-2. Answers will vary.
3. 30 x 3 = 90
4. 20 x 6 = 120
5. 45 x 2 = 90
6. 24 x 4 = 96
7. 8 x 10 = 80
8. 35 x 3 = 105
9. 12 x 6 = 72
10. 19 x 4 = 76

"Organ"ization! page 76

Name in top right.
1. lungs, nose–R
2. femur, ulna–S
3. aorta, vein–C
4. tendon, biceps–M
5. intestine, mouth–D
6. spinal cord, brain–N
7. artery, heart–C
8. humerus, radius–S
9. stomach, liver–D
10. ligament, triceps–M

Oddly Enough, page 77

1. ear, the others are part of the digestive system
2. hair, the others are all sense organs
3. biceps, the others are muscles
4. blood, the others are part of the skin
5. jaw, the others are parts of a tooth
6. hammer, the others are parts of the eye
7. lung, the others are blood vessels
8. ulna, the other bones are all in the head
9. lens, the others are parts of the ear
10. brain, the others all connect with bones in the skeletal system
11. liver, the others are part of the respiratory system
12. clavicle, the other bones are all in the arm
13. arteries, the others are parts of blood
14. rib, the others are joints
15. patella, the others are bones in the arm

Name at bottom.

Pre/Posttest, Part 6, page 78

Name in top right.
1. Mercury, Venus, Earth, Mars, Jupiter, Saturn, Uranus, Neptune, Pluto
2. blue
3. sun, Earth
4. about 1.5
5. M
6. S, M, E
7. E
8. ⑧ 25 60 400
9. meteor
10. black — hole black hole
    Milky — Way (Milky Way)
    asteroid — Comet solar eclipse
    solar — eclipse Halley's Comet
    Halley's — giant

Star Colors, page 80

- Antares 3000°C (red)
- Sun 6000°C (yellow)
- 7000°C
- 21,000°C (blue)

Name

Long Distance, page 82

Name in top left.

	Average Distance from the Sun		
Planet	A. Miles	B. Kilometers	C. Astronomical Units
Mercury	36,000,000	57,900,000	0.4
Venus	67,240,000	108,200,000	0.7
Earth	93,000,000	149,600,000	1.0
Mars	141,710,000	227,900,000	1.5
Jupiter	483,880,000	778,300,000	5.2
Saturn	887,140,000	1,427,000,000	9.5
Uranus	1,783,980,000	2,870,000,000	19.2
Neptune	2,796,460,000	4,497,000,000	30.0
Pluto	3,666,000,000	5,900,000,000	39.4

One astronomical unit is equal to the *distance* from the *Earth* to the *sun*.

Chart Check, page 83

1. Neptune
2. Venus
3. Saturn
4. Jupiter
5. Uranus and Neptune
6. 3,630,000,000
7. 78,300,000
8. Venus
9. Mars
10. Name

Which Body? page 84

Name in top left.
1. S
2. M
3. S, M, E
4. S
5. E
6. M, E
7. M, E
8. M
9. S
10. M, E
11. M, E
12. M
13. E
14. S
15. E

Sunny Numbers, page 87

Name in top right.
1. 865,000 miles
2. 93,000,000 miles
3. 8 minutes
4. 10,000°F
5. 35,000,000°F
6. 60
7. 175 miles per second
8. 25 days
9. 400
10. 193 years

Sunny Numbers, page 87

Name in top right.
1. SHOOTINGSTAR
2. HOOTINGTAR
3. HTINGTAR
4. HTEINGTAR
5. HTEINGTR
6. HTEINGTOR
7. HTEINTOR
8. HMEINTOR
9. HMENTOR
10. HMENTEOR
11. HMETEOR
12. METEOR

Astronomical Matchup, page 89

Name in top left.
1. asteroid belt
2. (Big Dipper)
3. [black hole]
4. dwarf star ★
5. Halley's Comet
6. meteor shower
7. Milky Way
8. northern lights
9. solar eclipse
10. sunspots
11. super giant ○